A Little Bit of Ivory

A Little Bit of Ivory

A Life of Jane Austen

Elfrida Vipont

Hamish Hamilton London

For Margaret

First published in Great Britain 1977
by Hamish Hamilton Ltd
90 Great Russell St, London WC1B 3PT

ISBN 0 241 89534 0

Photoset, printed and bound
in Great Britain by
REDWOOD BURN LIMITED
Trowbridge & Esher

. . . the little bit (two Inches wide) of Ivory on which I work with so fine a Brush, as produces little effect after so much labour.

Jane Austen to her nephew,
Edward Austen-Leigh.

ACKNOWLEDGEMENT

All the quotations from Jane Austen's letters contained in this volume are taken from *Jane Austen's Letters*, collected and edited by R. W. Chapman, 2nd edition, re-printed (with corrections) 1969, published by the Oxford University Press. The quotations from the *Juvenilia* are taken from *Jane Austen: Minor Works*, edited by R. W. Chapman, and published by the Oxford University Press in the Oxford Illustrated Jane Austen, 1969.

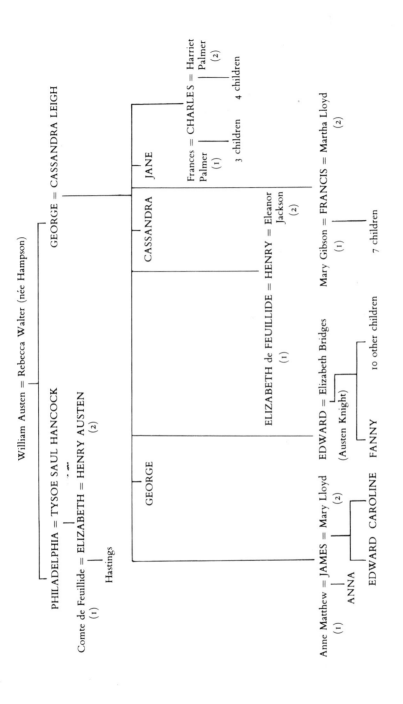

Prologue

To the best of my knowledge my great-great grandfather, William Curtis of Alton, never knew that he had a very important patient. Not that it would have made any difference to him if he had; as another of his descendants pointed out to me recently, he was not that kind of man.

William Curtis was a Quaker and came of an old-established Quaker medical family. His great-grandfather, grandfather and father had all practised medicine before him, and many of his descendants were to follow in the same profession. The name of the family is still preserved in Alton in the Curtis Museum, founded by his son, yet another William Curtis. The old Curtis house stands on the opposite side of the road to the museum, mellow and welcoming; there were still Curtises living in it when I was young.

William Curtis's important patient settled in the district with her mother and sister in 1809, in a little village called Chawton. It was a pretty enough place, with picturesque thatched cottages, but there were no buildings of any distinction save for the Manor, or the Great House, as it was generally called, and the village church. There seemed to be a general opinion that the village church was a shabby old building and ought to be re-built, but so far nothing much had been done beyond repairing it. Certainly it was unpretentious – the Great House was a far more imposing building – but it had served the people of Chawton for centuries, and generations of villagers had grown up within earshot of the three bells which rang out from its little square belfry, and been laid to rest under the great trees surrounding the churchyard.

The new patients moved into a house on the main road from London to Portsmouth. It was an attractive small house near the village pond, and their wealthy relatives, who lived at the Great House, had done much to make it suitable for them before they moved in. The most drastic change was to block up the drawing-room window, which looked out on to the road, and substitute one on the other side, thus ensuring greater privacy. The smaller parlour, which was the family sitting room and dining room, was left unaltered, so that passengers on the coaches as they clattered past could see the ladies seated round the table at their meals, if they so pleased. The elderly mother did not seem to mind this at all; sometimes she deliberately sat near the window for a while, so that she could watch the traffic going by. She liked it best of all when the coaches were packed with Winchester College boys going home on holiday; she had grandsons at Winchester, she told William Curtis proudly. Her own sons had been educated at home by their father.

William Curtis knew nothing of such schools as Winchester. They belonged to another world. He did not even plan to send his children to the great Quaker school at Ackworth, where his younger brothers and sisters had been among the first pupils. Yorkshire was a cold place for Hampshire-bred children and he preferred to keep his family at home.

Chawton was a very small place compared with Alton, which was a pleasant country town where something always seemed to be astir in those days, from French prisoners-of-war arriving (and sometimes escaping, to the great consternation of the inhabitants), to such local events as the annual fair on the Crown Close, opposite the Curtis house, which attracted people from miles around. It

2

is on record that at least one of the ladies from the cottage at Chawton enjoyed a visit to the Fair. They were all ladies: the elderly mother, her two unmarried daughters, and their friend, a Miss Lloyd, who lived with them.

The mother was a rather distinguished old lady, with an aristocratic nose of which she seemed inordinately proud. "Yes, we were a handsome family," she would say. "But my sister Jane was the beauty, not I. Only I have the family nose, and so has my daughter." She meant her elder daughter, who was certainly a pretty woman, with large dark eyes and a clear complexion. Anyone meeting her for the first time was bound to wonder how she could have been left a spinster, but there was a sad story of a young fiancé who went out to the West Indies as a Naval Chaplain and died there of yellow fever.

The mother was, of course, his chief patient. Her ailments were many and various, but it must often have surprised her medical attendant to come to the house when summoned in haste and find her digging potatoes in the garden, wearing her green gardening smock. The friend seemed a sensible woman, not particularly good-looking, but capable and understanding and kind. Watching her, one felt that she could have made somebody a good wife; perhaps the opportunity might come some day. The elder sister, her lost love locked down securely in her innermost heart, would look for no second flowering.

The younger daughter was, if anything, prettier even than her sister, though like her she tended to wear outmoded clothes and old-fashioned, old-maidish caps. Even William Curtis must have noticed this. His womenfolk wore the Quaker dress, as he did, but he had enough well-to-do patients to make him familiar with the changing fashions of the day. There would have been something slightly sad about these gentle ladies in their beautifully-made but dowdy dresses, had it not been for an inexplicable sense of vitality

3

in the house. Many things contributed to this. Young people were constantly coming and going, for the ladies were the centre of a large family circle; children seemed naturally to feel at home there, from the boisterous, who never failed to find something or somebody to amuse them, to the shy and timid, who never failed to find sympathy and understanding; visitors were always sure of a welcome and the ladies were never too busy or too preoccupied to entertain them. There was, however, one curious thing about the house. The door into the parlour creaked abominably. You could never enter quietly and unobtrusively, without disturbing the occupants. It seemed strange that one of the lady's sons or grandsons could not attend to the matter with a drop or two of oil. And yet perhaps something more subtle was involved. As the noise which had heralded your approach subsided, and you entered the room in a somewhat apologetic mood, you had a strange feeling as if something had stopped suddenly, as if life had stood still for a moment and then resumed its action upon a lower key. There was nothing to account for the sensation. The old lady would be sitting sewing placidly; the elder daughter and their friend would be reading or engaged on household tasks; the younger daughter would be rising from her little writing desk with a welcoming smile, as if this particular visitor was the one person she most of all longed to see.

It was a pity she did not seem to be as robust as her elder sister. There was nothing you could put your finger on. Indeed, she thought little of walking to Alton and back, and as a rule she looked better for the exercise. Yet there was always that indefinable something which can be sensed by an experienced practitioner. She never complained about her health. Her thought seemed to be always for her mother, and yet when the old lady launched into an account of her various ailments, there would be a lurking twinkle in her eyes, and an irrepressible curving of her lips.

4

This was a young lady with a sense of humour, but it was a sense of humour under strict control. Indeed her whole way of life seemed to be controlled, but the reason for that control remained an enigma.

William Curtis had many patients – rich and poor, wise and foolish, stoical and hypochondriacal. He attended them all with strict impartiality and Quaker rectitude. If he was curious about them, he did not pursue his curiosity, except in so far as the circumstances might affect their health; if he was more interested in some than in others, he never betrayed the fact. One thing might have surprised him, had he lived to see it. His family, settled in Alton for so many years, attracted in the course of time a degree of interest. Books were written about his famous cousin, William Curtis, the botanist, and also about his son, the founder of the Curtis Museum. And long after his body had been laid to rest in the little Friends' Burial Ground, near the seventeenth-century meeting house where he regularly worshipped, his own claim to fame was established. Beneath his honoured name in almost every version of the family tree, there is the description in varying terms: "medical attendant to Jane Austen". Unknown to himself, unsuspected by his immediate family, William Curtis, the Quaker apothecary of Alton, had a very important patient.

I

J ANE AUSTEN was born in 1775 at Steventon, a small village in Hampshire, about five miles from Basingstoke. It was a pleasant, quiet place, rather remote because of the bad state of the roads, which for the most part were nothing more than muddy country lanes. The village was set in pretty, undulating country, with fertile farms and fine old trees; there were few outstanding buildings in the neighbourhood, save for the great houses of the gentry here and there, and the little village churches. The great house at Steventon was a rambling Elizabethan manor belonging to Mr Thomas Knight, a distant relative of the Austens, and let to a farming family called Digweed, who only lived in part of it. The church was an unpretentious little building, dedicated to St Nicholas, and dating back to the twelfth century. As you pushed open the door, you could feel the almost tangible atmosphere of immemorial worship maintained for centuries. It was a typical village church, the heart of a worshipping community whose forbears slept in its shade. Between the church and the parsonage ran one of the double hedges with a path in the middle, which were characteristic of the Hampshire countryside; you might well be invisible as you walked between the thickly planted hedgerows, with tall trees on either hand, but you would hardly be inaudible, a situation which offered distinct possibilities to any budding novelist or dramatist who might walk there.

When the Reverend George Austen, Jane's father, first came to Steventon, he must have experienced a slight sinking of the heart. The parsonage was pleasantly situated, but it was a mere cottage, and the village itself had no possible claim to distinction. He had very little choice in the matter, of course. Almost all his life so far he had been a "poor relation", dependant on richer and well-disposed relatives for such preferment as came his way. He and his sister, Philadelphia, had been orphaned when very young. Their parents had not been well-to-do, and their future prospects must have seemed dim indeed. However, their wealthy uncle, Francis Austen, stepped in and took over the responsibility for the children. He himself was said to have set out as a youth to make his fortune, with a bundle of quill pens and £800, and made it very successfully.

The nephew, George, was a handsome, clever little fellow; he could surely be relied upon to make his way, given the right opportunities. He was sent to Tonbridge School, where he eventually fulfilled his uncle's expectations by winning an open scholarship to St John's College, Oxford. Philadelphia presented more of a problem. There was not much future for a portionless girl in those days; she might be as clever and wise and witty as she was undeniably beautiful, but the dreaded fate of a post as a governess seemed inescapably to lie ahead of her. From this fate her uncle saved her, with comparatively small expense to himself. The Mecca of portionless young ladies at that time was India, where there were plenty of young gentlemen sent out to make their fortunes with the East India Company, and a shortage of young ladies for them to marry. Accordingly Uncle Francis packed off his beautiful but impecunious young niece to Madras, where she fulfilled his hopes by attracting the attention of the English surgeon at Fort St David, a man considerably older than herself and of a

7

somewhat gloomy disposition, called Tysoe Saul Hancock.

George Austen continued to fulfil his uncle's expectations. When he came down from Oxford, he returned to Tonbridge School as a teacher and quickly rose to be Second Master. This was work he loved, for he was a born teacher, but doubtless his Uncle Francis considered he would be unlikely to make a fortune as a schoolmaster. It was surely a step in the right direction when he went back to Oxford in 1759, as a Fellow of St Johns. His outstanding good looks earned him the nickname of "the Handsome Proctor"; his features were regular, the lips firm and the eyebrows delicately arched, and his large eyes were of a brilliant hazel and unusually bright. His hair, which was thick and naturally curly, had gone white prematurely, and this gave him a very distinguished appearance, without in the least detracting from his good looks. He might be a poor relation, but he was a poor relation to be proud of. After he had taken Orders in 1760 it was not long before his future was assured through the good offices, first of his second cousin, Thomas Knight, who presented him with the living of Steventon, and then of his Uncle Francis, who added the living of Deane. Given the opportunity, he might have made his mark in some wealthy London parish, where his brains and his good looks and his gift for communicating knowledge might have enabled him to rise in the Church, but he was not over-ambitious and there is no doubt that, like the writer of the sixteenth psalm, he could say that his lines had fallen in pleasant places.

The parsonage at Steventon might not have been George Austen's idea of a "family house", but by the time he and his wife Cassandra came to live there, a few additions and alterations had transformed it into something which would certainly serve the purpose very well indeed. He had married Cassandra Leigh in 1764, at Walcot Church in Bath. In the opinion of his relations, he had done very well for himself. Miss Leigh came of a good family, better than his own; it is true she brought no fortune with her, but there was money in the family, so she might be said to have "expectations". Far more important, from George's point of view, were her delightful qualities. She was good-looking, though she insisted that her sister was the beauty of the family; she had a lively sense of humour; her practical gifts were considerable, and she loved the countryside. Nothing would have induced her to settle in London. When, later on, she visited relatives there, she was appalled by the noise and the dirt and the general hurly-burly. "Tis a sad place;" she said on her return. "I would not live in it on any account."

Mrs Austen's good family connections enabled the Austens and later their children, to maintain a nodding acquaintance with the local aristocracy. Not that Cassandra Austen showed any inclination to curry favour, or play the toady to the well-born. For a parson's wife in those days, she was unconventional in her behaviour. Before her marriage she had gloried in a scarlet riding habit, for which she would now have little use. She saw no reason for discarding a garment which became her so well, but wore it about the house, where it must have looked somewhat incongruous. Later on, it was cut up to provide hunting pink for her little sons. In no circumstances could she be tempted to play the fine lady; her growing family obviously necessitated an overflowing mending basket, and chance callers at the parsonage, high and low, would find her busy with her needle, mending little trousers and darning socks.

Away in India, Tysoe Saul Hancock shook his head over the prolific Austens. Writing to his wife, Philadelphia, who was on a visit to England at the time, he said: "I fear George will find it easier to get a family than to provide for them." By an irony of fate, his own godson, the second child, George, was the only one of the six Austen boys who would be unable to provide for himself. "Poor George" was to be the family secret. An epileptic, probably deaf and almost certainly weak-minded, he was to be cared for away from home for the rest of his life, but nobody knows how or where. The Austens were not callous; they would never have abandoned little George, or committed him to one of the grim institutions of the day; but they could not compromise the prospects of the other children. A defective child in the family circle was thought to be a shaming thing. Moreover, the Austens were already augmenting their income by taking in pupils, to live at the parsonage and be tutored by the Reverend George Austen; the poor little fellow would be a sad advertisement for such an establishment. The parents consoled themselves as best they could. "We have this comfort," wrote Mr Austen, when the boy was about four years old and even his mother, who had watched eagerly at first for signs of development, began to give up hope, "he cannot be a bad or wicked child." All his life, poor George was to be an "innocent".

Tysoe Saul Hancock might well shake his head. Child followed child at the parsonage in quick succession. The eldest, James, was born in 1765; he was supposed not to be very strong but he soon showed signs of being exceptionally bright for his age. Then came "poor George", then Edward, then Henry. Perhaps it was as well that Mrs Austen followed the contemporary fashion of "putting the children out to nurse"; they were weaned early and entrusted to a "good woman" in one of the neighbouring cottages, who fostered them until they were brought back into the family circle, after the birth of the next brother or sister. Meanwhile their parents visited them almost every day. The first girl, Cassandra Elizabeth, was born in 1773; she was a fascinating little thing, and as soon as she could talk would chatter all day long, so her mother said. On the whole, Mrs Austen was more interested in the boys, but she found little Cassy very entertaining at this stage. After

Cassandra came Francis, and then Jane, who was born in the bitterly cold December of 1775. Her parents had proved to be a month out in their reckoning, for they had expected her in November, but otherwise things went normally. Little Cassandra was naturally delighted to have a baby sister. Mr Austen did not think the little girls were at all alike. Cassy had big dark eyes like her brother, Edward, and she was fast developing her mother's distinctive nose; curly-haired Jane soon showed signs of inheriting her father's brilliant hazel eyes, like her brother Henry, though in his case the resemblance was even closer. From the first, the two little sisters were inseparable, except for the brief period when Jane was "put out to nurse". Curiously enough, each little girl was attracted to the brother she most resembled; Edward was Cassandra's "special brother" and Henry was Jane's.

Another boy, Charles, was born in 1779 – "our own particular little brother" his sisters called him, even after he had grown up. He was to be the youngest of the eight children – a big enough quiverful to send poor Dr Hancock into a melancholic decline had he lived to see it, but he died in the year Jane was born.

The Hancocks themselves had only one child, Elizabeth, born in 1761. Her godfather was the distinguished Warren Hastings, who had married a friend of her mother. Warren Hastings' wife had died when her baby girl was born; the infant died too, and Warren Hastings, almost inconsolable, gave his little daughter's name to his newborn godchild. His remaining child, three-year-old George, was so delicate that there seemed little chance of his surviving, especially in the climate of India, so when kind Philadelphia Hancock suggested two or three years later that the little boy be shipped back to England to be cared for by her brother, the Reverend George Austen, he felt she had saved his child's life.

Little George Hastings was George Austen's first pupil and Cassandra Austen's first nurseling, but to her great distress he died when he was six years old of what was then known as a "putrid sore throat"; this was a great killer in those days and probably approximated to diphtheria or typhoid. Young Mrs Austen was terribly upset. She had loved the child as if he had been one of the children she and her husband hoped soon to have. No blame was attached to the Austens. Warren Hastings continued to feel under an obligation to Dr and Mrs Hancock and to take an interest in his little god-daughter, on whom he had very generously settled the sum of £10,000, which was no small fortune for a child whose parents were not well-to-do. It enabled the widowed Philadelphia Hancock later on, after spending some years in England, to take her daughter to France to "finish" her education, and introduce her to the French Court at Versailles. It seemed quite another world from the one familiar to her cousins at Steventon, but Eliza remembered her uncle lovingly and sent him her portrait in miniature, wearing a fashionable white dress, trimmed with blue.

The Reverend George Austen continued to take in pupils to augment the family income. Sometimes they were very young, like little Lord Lymington, who came when he was six and seemed to be very happy. Mrs Austen proved to be good at mothering small boys. Sometimes they were sent because they were thought to be backward, like Master Vanderstegen, a pleasant, well-mannered boy who needed a good deal of individual tuition to bring him on. One boy, who came in 1779, Thomas Craven Fowle, was especially popular in the family circle; he was intended for a clergyman, and the Reverend George Austen was exceptionally good at preparing boys to enter university and to take Orders. Two boys, Richard Buller and William Goodenough, were long remembered for their complaints about the weathercock which creaked at night, so they said, and prevented them from sleeping. This was their favourite excuse when they overslept or were slow to understand their lessons. Mrs Austen wrote some nonsense verses for them – she was good at that kind of thing.

It whines and it groans and it makes such a noise
That it greatly disturbs two unfortunate boys,
Who hope you will not be displeased when they say,
If they don't sleep by night they can't study by day.

Everybody enjoyed Mrs Austen's sense of fun and her verses were preserved for years in the family circle.

The eldest of the Austen children, James, was obviously cut out to be a clergyman. No other career was to be considered for him. From the first he was a serious little boy, not very robust, perhaps, but studious and hard-working and responsible. His father was quite sure that for this pupil at least, no other teacher would be necessary. His hopes were justified, for James won a scholarship at the early age of fourteen and went up to his father's old college, St John's, Oxford, in 1779. Edward was quite another proposition. He was a delightful boy, much sturdier than his eldest brother and an adept at all country sports, but scholarly pursuits did not seem to attract him in the least. It was all the more exasperating because he was a highly intelligent child, as well as good-looking and attractive. His father wondered what would become of him if he could not be made to apply himself to his lessons. His mother did not seem to be unduly worried. She even encouraged their wealthy Knight relations to make a pet of him and carry him off to Godmersham Park, in Kent, for weeks on end. At first his father objected. How on earth was he going to make the child apply himself to his Latin grammar if he was to be indulged in this way? Mrs Austen looked at him with a twinkle in her eye. "I think, my dear, you had better oblige your cousins and let the child go," she said.

The fourth boy, Henry, was obviously cut out for another scholar; his proud father thought he had an even better brain than James, though he could be wayward if given the opportunity.

James was the born student, working for the love of it; Henry's may have been the more brilliant mind, but his interests were more varied and he found it hard to settle down and concentrate on the essential subjects, to the exclusion of all others.

All three boys were lively, good-tempered and energetic. They loved the open-air country life and rode, hunted and shot with enthusiasm, from a very early age. Such sports were not for little Cassandra, still under her mother's wing, but the next child, Francis, was a sportsman almost from the cradle. "Fly", as they called him when he was small, was a curly-headed little fellow, with a superabundance of charm which got him out of many a scrape, and a fund of sound commonsense which enabled him to hold his own and look after his own interests. Stories of him were handed down the family circle, especially the one about his pony, Squirrel, which he bought when he was seven for one pound eleven and sixpence and rode for two years, during which he taught him to jump pretty well anything he could "get his nose over", as he said. He then sold him for two pounds and twelve shillings. The family decided that Fly had a good eye for a bargain as well as a good seat on a horse.

It did not look as if Mr Austen would be able to make a scholar out of Francis, but he was inclined towards the sea rather than the Church at a very early age. However, as the schoolroom filled up with boys, their own and other people's, Mr and Mrs Austen were faced with a problem. Little Cassandra was no longer a baby; she was approaching ten and a highly intelligent little girl. She needed more teaching than her mother could give her, especially now that little Charles had returned from being "put out to nurse", but her father was fully occupied with the boys. Moreover, parents entrusting the education of their sons to the Reverend George Austen would not bargain for a little girl to be included amongst their fellow pupils. All kinds of complications could be envisaged, as Mrs Austen was quick to see. The last thing they could afford to do was to place any obstacle in the way of attracting pupils. They needed more, not less; it was a pity there were not more rooms at the parsonage.

It must have been at about this time that Mrs Austen's sister, the beautiful Jane Cooper, decided to send her daughter Jane to school at Oxford. This sounded an admirable arrangement. The school was kept by Mrs Cooper's sister-in-law, Mrs Cawley; it would not be like entrusting the child to strangers. The plan seemed so excellent that it occurred to the Austens that Cassandra might well accompany her cousin. Jane Cooper was slightly older than Cassandra and would be an ideal companion for her; moreover, she was a friendly, sweet-natured little girl and could be trusted to keep an eye on her and look after her. Only of course this would not free a bedroom at the parsonage, for the two sisters slept together. However, it would surely be cruel to part them. Little Jane was devoted to her elder sister; she followed her everywhere and was seldom happy for long without her. For Cassandra to go away to school would be a terrible blow; nobody could imagine how she would bear it, or even survive it. It would be much more sensible for the two little girls to go away together.

Jane was six years old. It was almost unthinkable to send a little girl away at such an early age, unless there were to be some very pressing reason. But of course there was a pressing reason. Not that the parsonage needed more room for pupils, but that the sisters could not be parted. It was then that Mrs Austen made one of her never-to-be-forgotten jokes. "If Cassandra were going to have her head cut off," she said, "Jane would insist on sharing her fate." It seemed irresistibly funny to the Austen boys. Even having your head cut off seemed funny; such things did not happen nowadays.

So, in 1782, after much family teasing, Jane, that funny little thing who would not be separated from her sister, set off for boarding school with Cassandra.

Mr Austen must have breathed a sigh of relief that at least he did not have to worry about his widowed sister and his pretty niece. Warren Hasting's £10,000 had paid handsome dividends. Eliza was now the wife of the Comte de Feuillide and a member of the French aristocracy. It was a far cry from the days when her mother, Philadelphia Austen, had been a poor relation. For Eliza, a glittering future seemed assured.

2

To very young children the decisions made in the adult world are, as a rule, almost completely incomprehensible. Naturally Jane would not be separated from Cassandra. Cassandra was her security, her shield, her protector against the outside world. For a sensitive child, it is an agonizing experience to be the butt of the family sense of humour. "If Cassandra were going to have her head cut off, Jane would insist on sharing her fate" – she heard this *ad infinitum* and *ad nauseam*, and nobody explained the joke. Of course she did not want to be separated from Cassandra. Of course she could not imagine life without her. But it is doubtful whether anybody explained to her that this meant going away from home at the age of six.

Most children accept what happens to them as a matter of course. They have no control over events, even the events which are to shape their lives. Few children have the precocious initiative of the little evacuee of the Second World War who wrote to his father: "Plese cum and fech me bak from this orful place." There can be no doubt that to Jane, Mrs Cawley's house in Oxford was an "orful place", and Mrs Cawley herself a strict and forbidding woman. There was to be none of the motherly care which Mrs Austen gave to the little boys in her charge, and none of the fun she shared with the older ones. But as for asking to be brought home, neither Jane nor even Cassandra would have dreamt of such a thing. So far as is known, they never complained, either at the time or afterwards. All that was left was an unhealed scar, a deep wound in the heart of the younger child, and this was only finally healed many years later when, in her novel *Mansfield Park*, she revealed to the world the sufferings of a little girl, exiled from her home to live among strangers, sufferings which she understood and entered into so fully that they live on to this day and create fresh heartache in succeeding generations. That little girl was called Fanny Price.

When Mrs Cawley moved from Oxford to Southampton, nobody questioned that Jane Cooper, and Cassandra and Jane Austen, and the other children should go with her. Why disturb the little girls when they were so happily settled? Indeed, one place must have seemed much the same to them as another. Mrs Cawley was the constant factor, and she was as strict and unprepossessing as before. When Cassandra and Jane developed sore throats, she made very little of it. She was particular in her care of the children; she looked after them in a way which satisfied the standards of her day, as well as her own conscience; but she did not believe in fussing over them or molly-coddling them when they complained of feeling poorly. Not that Cassandra and Jane complained; it was Jane Cooper who took fright.

Jane Cooper was a sensitive little girl and she was not as afraid of Mrs Cawley as the others were. After all, behind the stiff façade she was only an aunt, her father's sister, and not a very popular aunt at that. "Why don't you write to my mother or my aunt Cassandra?" she insisted. "Surely they would come?"

The last thing Mrs Cawley wanted was to have Mrs Cooper and Mrs Austen fussing round. The little girls only had putrid sore throats. Lots of children had putrid sore throats; it was a common ailment. True, some of them died of it, like poor little George Hastings, but she did not expect Cassandra or Jane to die. She could

18

look after them perfectly well and there was no need for anybody else to interfere.

Jane Cooper had none of her aunt's confidence. It seemed to her that little Jane Austen was very ill indeed, and if nothing more was done about it, she was as likely to die as any other child. Cassandra, struggling against a high fever, was terrified for her little sister. At last Jane Cooper took the law into her own hands. Reminding herself that Mrs Cawley was only an aunt and not a gorgon, she sent word to her mother surreptitiously and awaited the result.

Mrs Cawley's anticipations were justified. Mrs Cooper and Mrs Austen arrived with a minimum of delay, only by that time she was not sorry to see them. It really did look as if little Jane Austen was like to die. What Mrs Austen did not know about nursing sick children was hardly worth knowing. She took charge at once and pulled the child through against all expectations. Mrs Cooper, terrified of the infection, whisked her daughter away home with her to Bath. Perhaps she would have been wiser to stay where she was. Mrs Austen, fighting like a tiger for the life of her child, would have fought against all probabilities for the life of her dearly loved sister. For it was Mrs Cooper who caught the infection and took it home with her to Bath – Mrs Cooper who had been "the beautiful Miss Leigh" – and it was Mrs Cooper who died of it, leaving her family desolate, and her little daughter with a lifelong nagging memory at the back of her mind: "What would have happened if I had not sent word to Mama?"

The little girls would, of course, have to return to boarding school. So would Jane Cooper. They could not be entrusted to Mrs Cawley again, that at least was certain. But it seemed as if having them at home would create too much of an upheaval. Surely there was a school somewhere, kept by a motherly kind of person, where girls could scramble themselves into some kind of education without dying of neglect in the process.

19

Finally they were sent to Reading, which was then a pleasant country town, surrounded by flourishing market gardens; it might possibly suit them better than a bustling place like Southampton. Nothing much ever happened at Reading. It was of course the local market town and an important centre of the malting trade, but beyond that its main claim for consideration lay in the number of its excellent schools, from the Blue Coat School and the Grammar School to the innumerable private boarding schools which occupied many of the fine mansions along its principal streets. Reading was a very convenient place for this purpose. It lay on the main road from London to Bath, and at least three coaches came thundering in every day and deposited their passengers at The Crown for a hurried and expensive meal before resuming their journey. Reading might be an insignificant little town, but you were not sending your children out of your reach if you chose to send them to school there.

There were many academies for young gentlemen and they offered a wide choice; some specialized in the classics and prepared their pupils for Oxford or Cambridge, and some offered a more general education; some crammed the boys mercilessly like Dr Blimber's establishment in Dickens's *Dombey and Son* and a few did little more than keep the boys out of mischief. The young ladies' seminaries had little academic distinction, which, of course, was only to be expected. Many of them were intended for elegant young ladies, and the education they offered was meagre in the extreme. At such schools, even basic subjects like arithmetic were classed as "extras" and charged for accordingly, along with the fashionable accomplishments which were considered to be far more important for a young girl in those days. She might leave school without an idea in her head; she might be incapable of spelling or dealing with figures; but provided she could dance, and make her curtsey, and behave prettily, her education was to be considered completely satisfactory. Such an education, however, would hardly be suited to the needs of a country parson's daughters. Moreover, one consideration would surely be paramount. A school must be found for the little Austen girls where the pupils were well looked after so far as their health was concerned; nobody was prepared to risk another near-disaster. Here again, Reading could provide a ready answer. If you really wanted children to be well and happy, and did not insist on their heads being stuffed either with vanity or with a pretence of learning, the Abbey School was the place.

The Abbey School was kept by a stout, motherly lady with a cork leg, called Madame Latournelle. She was the widow of a Frenchman, and in spite of her name, could speak hardly a word of French. She was, however, very particular about the teaching of that language, and the girls at her school had a good grounding and learnt to speak it really well. It was not difficult at that time to obtain the services of a competent French master. Quite intelligent people seemed to be curiously apprehensive about the state of affairs on the other side of the Channel, and some of them were beginning to apply for likely positions which would enable them to establish themselves in England. It was probably all nonsense; the pretty Comtesse de Feuillide did not seem to notice anything amiss.

· The Abbey School occupied the old gatehouse of Reading Abbey and a large comfortable mansion adjoining it. There was a big old-fashioned garden, where the young ladies could walk and play in the summer, though it is doubtful whether the little ones would be allowed to roll down the grassy slopes as Jane loved to do in the garden at home. From the top of the embankment which bounded two sides of the garden you could look down on what remained of Reading Abbey, grey, shattered ruins hung about with ivy. Jane had not been brought up to regret the wholesale destruction of the monastic buildings of England, but she liked the old ruins well enough; people in those days were beginning to admire ruins as romantic and picturesque, and an embellishment to the landscape.

Madame Latournelle was no teacher, but she understood children. She believed in giving them plenty of good food and fresh air and exercise, and provided they attended to their lessons in the morning, they could do pretty well what they liked for the rest of the day. Above all, she was kind. Jane remembered years afterwards that in winter she dressed their chilblains with her own hands. Mr and Mrs Austen could at least be sure that no putrid sore throats would ever be neglected at the Abbey School.

The years spent at the Abbey School were comparatively uneventful. Nothing disturbed the easy, informal routine, save for the welcome, all-too-brief holidays spent at home, and the regular annual events, the end of term entertainments when the girls danced and sang and recited, and – even more exciting – the great Cheese Fair, when Dr Valpy's Grammar School boys were banished for a while from the Forbury, which served as their playing field, and the noise of the Fair broke in upon the customary quiet. The girls at the Abbey School surveyed the whole scene from their front windows; they could see the country people flocking in and watch the fun and games; they could even catch a whiff from the huge cheeses brought in from Cheddar and North Wiltshire and other parts of the country, which gave the Fair its name.

On one very rare occasion, the Austen girls and their cousin, Jane Cooper, had a special treat. Their brothers, Edward Austen and Edward Cooper were passing through the town with some of their friends, and the girls were allowed to dine with them at one of the local inns. This would have been unheard of in most establishments for young ladies at that time, especially as their brothers were not the only young gentlemen in the party, but easy-going

Madame Latournelle made no objection to the plan and the little girls had a red letter day. This must have been of especial importance to Cassandra, because Edward was her favourite brother, and it seemed inevitable that they were to be parted. Those frequent visits to his wealthy relations at Godmersham had borne fruit, for the Knights had adopted him as their heir and he was already spending more time with them than he did at home. There was to be no more hard, distasteful study for Edward; no longer would he have to spend long hours over his books under his father's watchful eye. The country sports he loved were to be his for the asking. He was not even expected to enter University, or to take Orders like James; instead, he would be making the Grand Tour, as other fashionable young gentlemen did, with plenty of money in his pockets, but with more common sense and far less vanity than most of them. George Austen could not make a scholar of Edward, but in the truest sense of the word he had succeeded in making a gentleman of him.

Edward was to be the traveller, but even quiet James seized an opportunity to go abroad when his cousin, Eliza de Feuillide, and her husband invited him to visit them in France. James was fascinated by Eliza. She and the Comte seemed to live in another world, so prosperous and happy and secure. Later in the year, Eliza and her mother came to England for the birth of her baby. The Comte seemed to have a curious idea that his child must be born in England, but whether this had some relation to his wife's fortune, or whether, if the baby were a boy, he wished to avoid any necessity for him to serve in the French army, or whether he was influenced by the rumours of social unrest, which did not seem to trouble his pretty little wife in the least, nobody seemed to know. Eliza and her mother settled in London, in a house in Orchard Street, and there the baby was born, a pretty, delicate little thing called Hastings after Eliza's famous godfather, who was even now being accused of such monstrosities of corruption as must inevitably lead eventually to his trial. Eliza and her mother did not believe a word of these accusations and neither did the Austens. The trial was to drag on for seven years and by the end of it Eliza's wealthy godfather, although acquitted, would be almost ruined.

Undoubtedly Eliza was able to enjoy the best of both worlds. Whether she was in London or in Paris, she made her appearance at Court; she curtsied to plain, kind-hearted Queen Charlotte, with her bevy of charming, discontented daughters and handsome, dissolute sons, and also to the French queen, Marie Antoinette, who always looked so elegant and self-assured; unlike the English queen, it seemed as if she had not a care in the world.

Fashionable and light-hearted Eliza might be, and in a fair way to having her head turned, but she never lost touch with her cousins at the parsonage in Steventon. She would descend on them like a little whirlwind of laughter and teasing and fun, flirting with the young men in a most charming manner, captivating the little boys, and winding her solemn uncle round her pretty little finger till he would agree with anything she suggested. Her shy little cousin, Jane, was fascinated by her and she had a special tenderness for the child. The elder girl, Cassandra, was sure of her position in the family, but Jane did not seem to be sure of anything or anybody. She lived in a world of her own and nobody appeared to be particularly interested in that world; only Eliza, unaware of its significance, but strangely attracted by her little cousin, would flash into it heedlessly yet lovingly, and awaken the sparkle in those large hazel eyes. Eliza adored her uncle and this funny little thing was strangely like him. She persisted in preferring her to Cassandra, which seemed to the rest of the family a very curious choice.

For a clergyman's family, the Austens seemed beyond measure enthusiastic about plays and all kinds of theatrical performances. There was very little opportunity to enjoy anything of the kind in quiet little Steventon, where young people must make their own entertainments or go without. Several members of the family had a marked gift for reading aloud, which was a very desirable pastime in those days, when the women of the family would stitch and embroider while one of their menfolk read aloud. Sometimes it would be the latest novel – the Austens were all keen novel readers – and sometimes it would be poetry or Shakespeare's plays. James and Henry were especially good at reading Shakespeare and could bring the characters to life in an admirable way. They were used to the idea of giving little performances in the home. The pupils would recite their pieces in the parlour before going home at the end of term; or the family would entertain one another with charades in the holidays, during the long winter evenings. It was no great step between this kind of little entertainment and acting a play, only inevitably before long their ambitions grew and the parlour seemed too small for a proper display of their talents. Eventually they migrated to the barn on the other side of the road; it was admirably suited for the purpose if only their father could be persuaded to fit it up with a stage and curtains.

By the time Cassandra and Jane left school, at an unusually early age (possibly when Jane was about ten), the barn "theatre" was in full swing. That Christmas, Eliza de Feuillide was the heart and soul of it all. She knew the very plays they must act: *Which is the Man?* and *Bon Ton*. She had seen them both with her mother and her cousin, Philadelphia Walter, at Tunbridge Wells. She herself would play a leading part, of course, but they were short of actresses. Philadelphia must be invited to join them, but "Phila" made short work of the idea. She did not want to appear in public, she said, but possibly her objection was more to appearing in public as second fiddle to Eliza. Between the Austens and their friends the problem was soon solved and the performance was pronounced to be a brilliant success. The parsonage was crammed to overflowing with lively young people; the barn was the scene of almost endless activity, with rehearsals and hilarious amateur scene-shifting and the assembling of "props"; and in the midst of it all, the little Jane, released from all fear of a return to school, wandered in and out, observing everything, fascinated by the activity and the fun, and occasionally warmed by a glance from the captivating Eliza, who knew every part in the play backwards and acted both on and off the stage, to the utter distraction of James and Henry, as she flirted impartially with each in turn.

Philadelphia Walter had refused to come. This fact probably stuck in Jane's memory and made her a little awkward when she first met her cousin "Phila". Mr and Mrs Austen had taken their two young daughters to visit relations in Kent and doubtless both girls were on their best behaviour. However, a sensitive child is inevitably aware of an attitude of criticism. Philadelphia warmed to Cassandra at once; for one thing, she was supposed to resemble herself, which was flattering, because everybody thought Cassandra very pretty. Jane must have sensed the preference. The awkward twelve-year-old became excessively awkward; she would push herself forward one moment and then lapse into an agony of shyness; she would talk too much and then refuse to say anything at all; and all the time those bright hazel eyes would be seeing everything, taking in everything, and revealing nothing.

"Jane is not at all pretty," decided Philadelphia Walter. "Jane is very prim, unlike a girl of twelve." Then, spurred on by the girl's unresponsiveness, she condemned her soundly. "Jane is whimsical and affected." She wrote as much to her cousin, Eliza de Feuillide, but the criticism slid like water off a duck's back. Nothing would ever persuade Eliza to give up her preference for Jane.

26

3

NOBODY SUGGESTED that Cassandra and Jane should be sent to France, like their cousin Eliza, to "finish" their education. They had, of course, no wealthy benefactor. Even if the money had been available, however, Mr Austen would not have approved. His doubts about the value of a French education had crystallized into a positive dislike of Eliza's marriage to a Frenchman, even though it transformed her into a countess; he feared it might lead to his sister Philadelphia and her daughter Eliza "giving up their friends, their country and their religion". In any case, he preferred to educate his children at home. He did not even follow the usual custom and engage a governess; he had engaged no tutor for his sons, and they had all done him credit, though his brilliant son, Henry, had not in the event emulated the outstanding success of his firstborn, James; he entered St John's at the age of seventeen, not at fourteen like his elder brother. He was, however, very popular, though he seemed to have experienced some difficulty in settling down.

There was no question of a classical education for the girls. By no possible stretch of the imagination could this be considered necessary, or even desirable. They had left boarding school with the average accomplishments of the day. They spoke French well and had a smattering of Italian, and they had been taught to cultivate a beautifully neat and legible handwriting, with the same artistic quality as their exquisite needlework. Jane's spelling left much to be desired, but doubtless this would right itself, as she read more widely. Reading was the most important thing in education; Mr Austen had an excellent library and he turned the girls loose in it, with no restrictions of any kind.

Like most sensitive, imaginative children, Jane had a world of her own to which she could retreat at will. Books were part of that world, but she was not "bookish" in the conventional sense. Everything she experienced was part of that world, but it did not belong to the world of everyday. The stories she invented were part of that world, but they were not meant to be taken seriously. Like Henry, she had an irrepressible sense of humour, and once she was safely back in her own home, she let it have full swing, all the more so because she had suppressed it for so long. There had been very little fun in the shadow of Mrs Cawley, and even the easy, uneventful life at the Abbey School had been shot with homesickness. Now there was no need to keep the brake on any longer, and Jane's inherent liveliness could bubble up into mischief without any serious consequences, though it is doubtful whether her father was best pleased when he found the "sample" marriage forms in his parish registers filled in neatly with particulars of his younger daughter's marriages to various wholly imaginary young gentlemen.

Reading aloud was still one of the greatest pleasures in the family circle. They might sometimes amuse themselves with rhymed charades or riddles, but nearly every evening would find them in the parlour, Mrs Austen and the girls busy with their needles, and Mr Austen or one of his sons reading some recently-published novel from the circulating library, or possibly one of the classical authors whose works were part of the education of the younger ones. Soon only Cassandra, Jane and Charles were permanently at home;

James was at Oxford, where Henry joined him in 1788; Edward now lived with his benefactors, the Knights; and Francis was at the Royal Naval Academy in Portsmouth. All four brothers only came home occasionally, when on vacation or on leave. Francis was soon far away from home, for he was so successful in his studies at the Naval College that he had a chance to volunteer for the East Indies in 1788. Nevertheless, they were all at home sufficiently often for the young people to get a great deal of fun out of their novel-reading. They read all they could lay hands on, good, bad and indifferent, and while they developed a sound appreciation of the best, they enjoyed making mock of the others – all those fainting young ladies and distracted young gentlemen sent the whole family into gales of laughter. Jane had her own way of making fun of them. She would mimic them in mock sentimental stories, which she wrote down in that exquisite hand of hers and prefaced with a pompous dedication to some member of the family. Some of these stories still exist, brimful of nonsense and intended to be regarded as such. Jane would read them to Cassandra, and the two sisters would giggle delightedly at the preposterous mimicry. Cassandra could be wholehearted in her admiration, for she had no desire to enter into competition with Jane. Her own gifts were for drawing and painting and these she did superlatively well, in the opinion of the whole family. Perhaps she would be a real artist some day. In any case, hers was a talent to be taken seriously, whereas Jane's was little more than an ephemeral knack for creating nonsense.

At first nothing was intended except mockery. It was fun to turn all those grandiose descriptions of captivating young ladies inside out, and describe the "forbidding squint and the greasy tresses" of a "lovely and too charming Fair One", or to exaggerate to the point of absurdity the good looks of some hero "of so dazzling a beauty that none but Eagles could look him in the Face". She mockingly described "the beams that darted from his Eyes" as so strong that "none dared venture within half a mile of them" until "the gentleman at last finding the feirceness of his beams to be very inconvenient to the concourse . . . half shut his eyes".

Sudden bosom friendships between families were fair game. The intimacy between three imaginary families "daily increased until it grew to such a pitch that they did not scruple to kick one another out of the window on the slightest provocation". One young lady is addicted to drink and assures her friend that "except for her Father and Brother, Uncles, Aunts, Cousins and Other Relations, Lady Williams, Charles Adams, and a few dozen more of particular friends, she loves her better than almost any other person in the world". The writer adds: "Such a flattering assurance of her regard would justly have given much pleasure to the object of it had she not plainly perceived that the amiable Alice had partaken too freely of Lady Williams' claret." This is the eighteenth century, not the Victorian era: the child of the parsonage describes a whole party being "carried home dead drunk", and explains that some of her characters, "though a little addicted to the Bottle and the Dice, had many good Qualities", but even her father makes no attempt at censorship.

Obviously, Jane was enjoying herself. She invented ridiculous place names – "Crankhumdunberry", "Pammydiddle" and "Kilhoobery Park" – and she revelled in mocking the fainting habits of the young ladies in popular romances. "She accordingly fainted and was in such a hurry to have a succession of fainting fits, that she had scarcely patience enough to recover from one before she fell into another." Her characters tell their life stories on the slightest provocation and almost always with a nonsensical twist. Lady Williams describes her "excellent Governess":

"She instructed me in the Paths of Virtue, and might perhaps by this time have nearly attained perfection, had not my worthy Preceptoress been torn from my arms, ere I had attained my seventeenth year. I shall never forget her last words. 'My dear Kitty,' she said, 'Goodnight t'ye.' I never saw her afterwards," continued Lady Williams wiping her eyes, "she eloped with the Butler the same night."

Like many young writers, Jane Austen would sometimes fail to finish her stories. She began one about Sir William Montague, an engaging young gentleman who, after falling in love with three young ladies at once, "became enamoured of a young Widow of Quality", but could not marry her because she insisted on fixing a date for the wedding which clashed with the opening of the shooting season. This promising romance was dedicated to Charles but she either tired of it or ran out of ideas, for she broke off suddenly and never finished it. Charles must have protested, for she followed it up with another also dedicated to him. It was about a wealthy young man who owned "a Coach, a Chariot, a Chaise, a Landau, a Landaulette, a Phaeton, a Gig, a Whiskey, an Italian Chair, a Buggy, a Curricle and a wheelbarrow". This also was to be "an unfinished tale", which seems a pity, for one would like to know more about the young man who sought to "comfort himself with a good hot supper and therefore ordered a whole Egg to be boiled for him and his servants". Both these fragments have a flavour of impromptu stories told at bedtime to her "own particular brother", Charles. Possibly they may have been written down at his instigation.

The family enjoyed Jane's nonsense stories, just as they enjoyed Mrs Austen's nonsense rhymes. There was nothing more to it than that, except possibly in the case of her eldest brother, the rather solemn James. Many years later, he took some pride in the idea that he, as well as their father, had contributed a little to her education.

31

His son, Edward Austen-Leigh, wrote in his memoirs of Jane Austen that his father had "a large share in directing and forming her taste". It seems that James had some literary aspirations, for when he was at Oxford he founded a magazine called *The Loiterer* and contributed many of the articles himself. Early in 1789, however, a contribution appeared which could by no stretch of the imagination be attributed to James, or even to his brother Henry, who had recently joined him at Oxford. Henry was a clever, witty youth, but a pedantic writer. This was not an article but a letter, signed with an obvious pseudonym, *Sophia Sentiment*. The young lady protests at the sombre character of the magazine and pleads for a little variety.

> Let us see some nice, affecting stories, relating the misfortunes of two lovers, who died suddenly just as they were going to church. Let the lover be killed in a duel, or lost at sea, or you may make him shoot himself, just as you please; and as for his mistress, she will of course go mad; or if you will, you may kill the lady and let the lover run mad; only remember, whatever you do, that your hero and heroine must possess a great deal of feeling and have very pretty names.

There is no possible reason for suspecting that Jane could have written this and every reason to suppose that she did, but there is no evidence either way. The letter ends with the dire threat that if her suggestions are not carried out, "may your work be condemned to the pastry cook's shop and may you always continue a bachelor with a maiden sister to keep house for you".

Whatever the truth of the matter may be, there can be no doubt that this letter must have occasioned many sisterly giggles in the rooms shared by Cassandra and Jane at the parsonage at Steventon.

There was no lack of space at the parsonage now, and no need to send any members of the family away to make room for others.

Cassandra and Jane shared two rooms on the first floor, a small bedroom and a larger dressing room which served as their sitting room. There was ample space for all their ploys. Cassandra could draw and paint to her heart's content, and Jane could scribble away at her writing desk, or play the piano without disturbing the rest of the family. They could also entertain their friends, for even in this rather remote country village there were young ladies within reach who could be relied on for a friendly visit and a chat. Chief among these were the Miss Lloyds, who had come to live in the neighbouring village of Deane. Their widowed mother had rented the rectory, which stood just opposite Deane House, the home of the Harwood family, to whom the young people of the neighbourhood were much indebted on account of their addiction to giving dances in their beautiful ballroom. Deane, very close to Steventon, was Mr Austen's second living, presented to him by his wealthy Uncle Francis, and on this account there was no resident rector.

There were three Lloyd sisters, Martha, Eliza and Mary. Eliza was already married to her cousin, the Reverend Fulwar Craven Fowle, elder brother to Tom Fowle, who had been one of the Reverend George Austen's pupils. Tom had been a general favourite at the parsonage and they had never lost touch with him. Martha and Mary were pleasant, good-humoured girls, though Martha was the more easy-going of the two; Jane dedicated one of her first nonsensical stories to her. The story was called *Frederick and Elfrida*, and the dedication was the only serious part of it. "My dear Martha," it ran, "as a small testimony of the gratitude I feel for your late generosity to me in finishing my muslin Cloak, I beg leave to offer you this little production of your sincere Freind the author." Jane could never remember which came first, the "i" or the "e"; she was to be unsure about this, and other little matters concerning spelling, for the rest of her life.

33

Mrs Lloyd was a quiet, sweet-natured lady, and the girls were friendly and pleasant, though not particularly good-looking. There was nothing to suggest a skeleton in the family cupboard, and yet behind that attractive household lay the shadow of a notorious scandal. Mrs. Lloyd's mother had been the "cruel Mrs. Craven", a beautiful, fashionable but infamous lady, who had treated her three daughters abominably, starving them, beating them, and locking them up, until in desperation they took advantage of her temporary absence and ran away from home, two of them to be married and one, the future Mrs Lloyd, to take refuge with kindly relatives. The story haunted Jane. Eventually she would have to write it out of her mind before she could see things in proportion again.

Other close friends of the Austen girls were three sisters, Elizabeth, Catherine and Alethea Bigg, who lived at Manydown House, near Basingstoke. When Cassandra and Jane were old enough to attend the balls held at the Assembly Rooms of the Angel Inn at Basingstoke, they used to spend the night at Manydown House. The family were more generally known as the Bigg-Withers, because their father had assumed the hyphenated name of "Bigg-Wither" on receiving an inheritance, and had adopted it for his little son, Harrison. The girls, however, preferred to retain the simple surname of Bigg.

An older, dearly-loved friend of the Austen sisters was the charming young Mrs Lefroy – or Madame Lefroy as she was often called – wife of the Reverend Isaac Lefroy, Rector of Ashe. The Lefroys had come to Ashe while Cassandra and Jane were away at school; Mr Lefroy had succeeded Mr Russell, the former rector, whose daughter, Mrs Mitford, was to say some spiteful things about Jane Austen, describing her as "the prettiest, silliest, husband-hunting butterfly" that she could remember. It may be that she was jealous of the Austens, that brilliant, lively family of young people who seemed – the boys at least – to be so very sure of themselves. On the contrary, the Lefroys were very fond of Mr and Mrs Austen and their children, and Mrs Lefroy took a special interest in Jane, which called out the girl's best qualities. It was a most happy friendship and it proved to be a formative influence in Jane's life, but at this stage it must have seemed far more important to Jane that the Lefroys attracted young people to their rectory like bees to a honeypot, and were prepared to open the folding doors between two of their rooms so that they might enjoy informal dances. There was no standing on ceremony; it did not matter whether younger sisters were considered to be "out" or not. All their kind host and hostess wanted was to see them enjoy themselves. Jane's shyness broke down in this lively, kindly atmosphere. She loved dancing, and she loved music, and she loved pretty clothes, even if she had contrived them herself out of "hand-downs". It may possibly have added to her enjoyment that people were beginning to think that she was pretty.

She was still writing nonsense stories. In 1790, before her fifteenth birthday, she attempted a more ambitious one and carried it through successfully. This was something more than those unfinished fragments, or even the completed ones, which seldom ran to more than a few pages and ended abruptly when the fun ran out. This was a burlesque but it was also, in its own way, a work of art. The title was *Love and Freindship* – no amount of study, and no painstaking efforts made by her father and her brother, James, would ever correct Jane's spelling. The dedication was to "Madame la Comtesse de Feuillide", and Eliza must have appreciated it more than most. She was spending more time in England now, owing to the disturbed state of affairs in France. During the previous year the Bastille had fallen, and starving women had marched to Versailles to fetch the royal family back to Paris. It seemed a far cry from the days when Eliza de Feuillide had curtsied to Marie Antoinette in the Palace of Versailles, where everything had seemed so secure and the secret anxieties of many people, including her worried husband, so utterly ridiculous. Things would settle down eventually, of course, and meanwhile Eliza enjoyed life in England.

Like many novels of the period, though the fashion was not quite as popular as it had been, *Love and Freindship* was told in a series of letters, mainly written by the principal character, Laura, to the daughter of her intimate friend. Laura introduces herself to the young Marianne in a paragraph which no more suggests the "prim" little Jane Austen than it does the daughter of a country parson. "My Father was a native of Ireland and an inhabitant of Wales; My Mother was the natural Daughter of a Scotch Peer by an italian Opera-girl — I was born in Spain & received my Education at a Convent in France."

In this story there are scenes reminiscent of the theatre or the early opera. For instance, when a stranger knocks again and again at a cottage door, it takes a whole letter to elucidate the mystery.

My Father started — "What noise is that," (said he.) "It sounds like a loud rapping at the Door" — (replied my Mother.) "it does indeed." (cried I.) . . . "Had we not better go and see who it is? (said she) the Servants are out." "I think we had." (replied I.) "Certainly, (added my Father) by all means." "Shall we go now?" (said my Mother.) "The sooner the better." (answered he). "Oh! let no time be lost." (cried I.) A third more violent Rap than ever again assaulted our ears. "I am certain there is somebody knocking at the door." (said my Mother.)

The speculation speeds back and forth, for all the world like the characters in a late seventeenth- or early eighteenth-century opera, spinning out the action to fit the ravishing music of Purcell or Handel.

There are also scenes which strike a more recent note, suggesting that the rebellion of the younger generation is not a modern invention.

My Father, seduced by the false glare of Fortune and the Deluding Pomp of Title, insisted on my giving my hand to Lady Dorothea. No never exclaimed I. Lady Dorothea is lovely and Engaging: I prefer no woman to her; but know Sir, that I scorn to marry her in compliance with your wishes. No! never shall it be said that I obliged my Father.

The fainting young ladies of those popular romances enjoyed and laughed over by the young Austens are duly mocked when Laura and Sophia faint "alternately on a Sofa". In a later incident, the young ladies find an overturned phaeton with "two gentlemen most elegantly attired but weltering in their blood", who prove to be their husbands, Edward and Augustus. "Sophia shrieked and fainted to the Ground — I screamed and instantly ran mad." Sophia catches a chill after lying on the damp ground, and her dying advice to Laura contains the warning: "beware of swoons dear Laura — a frenzy fit is not one quarter so pernicious; it is an exercise to the Body and if not too violent, is I dare say conducive to Health in its consequences — Run mad as often as you chuse; but do not faint."

None of this was to be taken seriously, of course, any more than Jane's writing in itself was to be taken seriously. It was all part of the family fun, to which everybody contributed in one way or another.

It was a pity that the last of the fledglings were leaving the nest. Charles was due to enter the Royal Naval Academy in 1791, and after that only the girls would be at home. They too would leave when the time came for them to be married. There was no doubt about that, of course. Eliza de Feuillide said they were "two of the prettiest girls in England".

Fifteen-year-old Jane was beginning to try out other ideas. In 1791, she embarked on a *History of England from the reign of Henry the 4th to the death of Charles the 1st; by a partial, prejudiced and ignorant Historian*. She dedicated it to Cassandra, with an encouraging foot-note: "N.B. There will be very few Dates in this History." Cassandra entered into the fun wholeheartedly, and added some illustrations of her own to embellish the work. They were neatly executed portraits of sovereigns in roundels, in imitation of the ones used in Goldsmith's *History of England*. The girls must have enjoyed many a laugh over this historical work in that dressing room upstairs, with the dingy carpet and the painted furniture. Needless to say, Jane was not "ignorant", but she was certainly "partial" and "prejudiced" to her own great satisfaction. Like the rest of the family, she had been made to study Oliver Goldsmith's *History of England* as a lesson book, and when unable to restrain her-self, she would write notes in the margin. "Oh! Oh! the Wretches!" was her comment on Cromwell and his supporters.

The opening paragraph of Jane's *History* set the tone for the whole. "Henry the 4th ascended the throne of England much to his own satisfaction in the year 1399, after having prevailed on his cousin and predecessor Richard the 2nd to resign it to him, and to retire for the rest of his life to Pomfret Castle, where he happened to be murdered." The humour here is delicately balanced. Jane had outgrown the childish mockery of those·"greasy tresses" and the "forbidding squint"; she now commented wryly on events and motives. The only thing to be said in vindication of Henry VIII was that his "abolishing Religious Houses and leaving them to the ruinous depredations of time, has been of infinite use to the land-scape of England in general, which probably was a principal motive for his doing it since otherwise why should a Man who was of no Religion for himself be at so much trouble to abolish one which had for Ages been established in the Kingdom".

Lady Jane Grey was twice referred to as "reading Greek" when other people were seeking more obvious pleasures, but Jane, little given to any kind of blue-stocking complex herself, wondered "whether she really understood that language or whether such a Study proceeded only from an excess of vanity for which I believe she was always rather remarkable". She found Mary, Queen of Scots, irresistible – "this Bewitching princess whose only freind was then the Duke of Norfolk, and whose only ones now are Mr. Whitaker, Mrs. Lefroy, Mrs. Knight and myself " – and she flatly refused to accept any evidence against her, or to listen to a word of those she vilified as the enemies of her idol. Indeed, her picture of Mary Queen of Scots owed something to her youthful admiration for Eliza de Feuillide and for Mrs Lefroy.

With the accession of the Stuarts, the vein began to run out. Writing history was fun, but you were in some measure fettered by the past, though Jane did not hesitate to prophesy a worthy successor to Sir Francis Drake in the person of her brother Francis, now at sea.

It was about this time that Sir Francis Drake the first English Navigator who sailed round the world, lived, to be the ornament of his Country and his profession. Yet great as he was, and justly celebrated as a Sailor, I cannot help forseeing that he will be equalled in this or the next Century by one who tho' now but young, already promises to answer all the ardent and sanguine expectations of his Relations and Freinds, amongst whom I may class the amiable Lady to whom this work is dedicated, and my no less amiable Self.

This passage may have pleased Jane's father, but it is doubtful whether he would have approved of a paragraph in the following chapter, which was devoted to the reign of James I. "As I am myself partial to the roman catholic religion, it is with infinite regret that I am obliged to blame the Behaviour of any Member of it; yet Truth I think being very excusable in a Historian, I am necessitated to say that in his reign the roman Catholics of England did not behave like Gentlemen to the protestants." From a daughter of an eighteenth-century parsonage, this expression of partiality for "the roman catholic religion" is surprising. In other ways Jane was very much a child of her time, and a paragraph in the same chapter might have given occasion for a few raised eyebrows in later generations. James I was in Jane's opinion "of that amiable disposition which inclines to Freindship", and she added: "I once heard an excellent sharade on a Carpet, of which the subject I am now on reminds me . . . my first is what my second was to King James 1st and you tread on my whole." Obviously the relationship between James I and Robert Carr was no mystery to the young Jane Austen.

Probably Jane was not sorry to write "finis" on 26 November 1791, when she reached the end of Charles I. It would have been difficult to have sustained the nonsense any further. There was, however, more to it than that. During the same year Jane had been working on other ideas, at first very light-heartedly. Probably she intended to produce no more than another set of nonsense stories to be laughed over in the family circle. She prefaced them by a delicious mock dedication to her cousin, Jane Cooper. "Cousin, Conscious of the Charming Character which in every Country, and every Clime in Christendom is Cried Concerning You, with Caution and Care I commend to your Charitable Criticism this Clever Collection of Curious Comments, which have been Carefully Culled, Collected and Classed by your Comical Cousin The Author."

It was a collection of letters, written separately and individually by different imaginary characters. These letters are all fragments, but each tells a story, and into each at some stage life breaks in and the characters are no longer puppets or figures of fun, but living people with minds of their own. Nevertheless some of the letters still subside happily into the mockery. A young man writes "How ardently I hope for the death of your villainous Uncle and his Abandoned Wife, Since my fair one will not consider to be mine till their decease has placed her in affluence above what my fortune can procure," adding hopefully "Though it is an improvable Estate." At a later stage the same young man exclaims "with Virulence against Uncles and Aunts" and hurls accusations against the laws of England "for allowing them to possess their Estates when wanted by their Nephews and Neices".

This fun may have been rather too near the bone to be appreciated by the older members of the family circle, who in former days had depended very much upon the generosity of uncles and aunts for their advancement, and who now looked to their relations for help in furthering the prospects of their numerous brood. Thanks to the Knights, Edward was already established, and they had long looked to Mrs Austen's prosperous brother, James Leigh Perrot, to ensure James's future by making him his heir. They may well have felt that it ill became Jane to make fun of uncles and aunts. On the other hand, nobody had suggested that any particular consideration should be given to Cassandra and Jane.

One story in *A Collection of Letters* is not funny at all. The other members of the family may have laughed over it as another scrap of Jane's delicious nonsense, but if so, they must have been skating over very thin ice. It purports to be a letter "from a young Lady in distress'd Circumstances to her freind", and the "young Lady" is a pretty girl, Maria Williams, who has been invited to a ball. Her mother, who never goes out, cannnot chaperon her, so she entrusts her to the care of Lady Greville, who has two daughters of her own. The poor child knows she will be the butt of Lady Greville's scorn but dares not protest, for her mother thinks the connection too valuable to be sacrificed. The miserable ride in Her Ladyship's coach is described in vitriolic detail. The girl's pretty new dress immediately attracts attention: "Why could not you have worn your old striped one? It is not my way to find fault with people because they are poor, for I always think they are more to be despised and pitied than blamed for it, but at the same time I must say that in my opinion your old striped gown would have been quite fine enough for its wearer." The nagging continues until they alight at the grand house where the ball is being held, but is resumed when, to Lady Greville's indignation, Maria attracts the attention of a very eligible young man. "Pray, Miss Maria," enquires her Ladyship in ringing tones, "in what way of business was your grandfather?" and she proceeds to make all manner of scornful suggestions, which Maria parries in such a spirited way that afterwards she fears lest she may have been thought "too saucy". The persecution ceases only because Lady Greville finds somebody better to talk to, but she takes her revenge next day, when she calls at Maria's home at their unfashionable dining hour, and insists on summoning Maria out into the bitter wind, to stand at the coach door and be scolded. "You are used to be blown about by the wind, Miss Maria, and that is what has made your complexion so raddled and coarse," she observes. Maria dares not protest or answer back, but her reaction is still spirited. When Lady Greville invites her to dine with them the day after tomorrow – not tomorrow when they have important guests – and tells her that she will not send the carriage for her – "if it rains you may take an umbrella" – the girl writes that she "can hardly help laughing at hearing her give me leave to keep myself dry".

However, this is no laughing matter, except for those who can bring themselves to laugh when the feelings of a sensitive child are trampled on and exposed. This letter is the sole surviving piece of evidence to suggest that at this time, before she was equipped to deal with it, Jane encountered snobbery and was wounded by it. Later on, she would learn to grow a second skin; later on she would be able to transmute such an experience with a delicate and delicious wit into a shaft of ridicule to pierce the thickest hide; now she was a young girl, sheltered by a happy, loving family circle and surrounded by friendly neighbours, who had been suddenly confronted by a cold blast from the outside world against which she was defenceless. Only she would not continue defenceless. For the rest of her life she would give snobbery – whether of birth or wealth or of pretension – no quarter.

4

THE STATE OF AFFAIRS in France seemed to be growing rapidly worse. The Comte de Feuillide brought his wife and their delicate little son back to England in 1791; obviously they would have to remain there until things settled down, but meanwhile he thought it better to return to France and keep an eye on his property. After all, he was no fool; he knew how to look after himself. So did Eliza. She was perfectly happy until her mother died, when she was so distraught and inconsolable that her husband had to come rushing back to comfort her. He might have been tempted to stay indefinitely, had it not been for the risk of losing his property. If you were declared an *emigré*, then all your possessions were confiscated, and this was something which neither he nor Eliza could face. How could he contemplate starting life all over again, with no resources, in an alien country? He could not stay for ever with his wife's poor relations at Steventon. And what would become of the charming Comtesse, so admired by everybody, so accomplished at breaking hearts and tenderly putting them together again? She had not married a French aristocrat to become a nobody, like the rest of her family. She kissed her husband goodbye and embraced her little son as his kind *papa* rode away. He would soon come riding back and then they would be able to cross the Channel in a big boat and live in France again, and everything would be as it used to be.

Meanwhile there were changes at the parsonage. The eldest son, James, had left Oxford and was now curate of the parish church at Overton, about six miles away from home. The tenants of the great house, General Matthew, and his wife, Lady Jane, were very kind to the young man; he might be over-serious, but he was intelligent and sincere and well-mannered, and an excellent acquisition as a curate. They frequently invited him to the house, where he soon felt so thoroughly at home that he lost much of his shyness and apparent awkwardness. It was not long before Anne, the daughter of the house, fell in love with him, and he with her. She was five years older than he was and inclined to be delicate, but it seemed that the young couple were suited to one another, though not equally matched in fortune. Both fathers did what they could; General Matthew gave his daughter an allowance of a hundred pounds a year, which was a considerable sum in those days, and Mr Austen gave up the living at Deane, which he had held with Steventon. This in its turn brought changes into life at the parsonage, for Mrs Lloyd and her daughters would have to give up the tenancy of their dearly-loved home to make way for young Mr and Mrs Austen.

At first the girls of both families were almost inconsolable. What would Cassandra and Jane do when they could no longer run over to Deane to share the latest gossip, or study the fashions, or chatter about dances and the people who had attended them? And what would Martha and Mary do when they were no longer free of the parsonage, where they had been like members of the lively Austen family of boys and girls? Nothing would ever be the same again. Cassandra may have secretly wondered how she and Tom Fowle could keep up their friendship now that he would no longer be a frequent guest at Deane.

In the event, the Lloyds only moved to Ibthorpe, which was

about twenty miles away. The families were not inexorably parted, but the old free and easy relationship was no longer possible. Jane made a tiny chintz housewife as a parting gift for Mary and fitted it up with fine needles and thread; it was such a perfect thing in its way that Mary kept it, just as it was, and so it has been preserved to this day. It contains a scrap of paper with a minute inscription:

This little bag, I hope, will prove
To be not vainly made;
For should you thread and needle want,
It will afford you aid.

And as we are about to part,
Twill serve another end;
For when you look upon this bag,
You'll recollect your friend.

It was just such a jingle as her mother might have written.

It seemed as if there was a positive epidemic of weddings in the family at this time. James and his Anne were married in March and in the previous December Edward had been married to a lovely girl, Elizabeth Bridges, daughter of Sir Brook Bridges of Goodneston, a man of very considerable property. Nothing could have better pleased his wealthy adoptive parents. The adoption had been a complete success: Edward had never given them a moment's anxiety and now he had chosen a bride of good family, well known to them, in fact the very bride they would have chosen for him had the choice been theirs – which it quite probably was. The young couple went to live at a house called Rowling in West Kent, not far from Elizabeth's former home. They were warm in their invitations to Edward's sisters to come and stay with them; Elizabeth was young and pretty and friendly, and she looked forward to entertaining her sisters-in-law.

Yet another wedding took place before the year was out, this time actually in Steventon. Jane Cooper had kept up her friendship with the Austen cousins ever since they had been at school together; when her father died during the summer, it was the most natural thing in the world for her to take refuge with her uncle and aunt. She was already engaged to be married to Captain Thomas Williams RN, and in December she was married from the parsonage at Steventon. Captain Williams was a very desirable addition to the family from the point of view of the sailor brothers; it was all very well trying to win promotion by your own merit, but there was nothing like a word in high places to give you a push up the ladder. For some years Francis and Charles were to owe many of their opportunities for advancement in their careers to Captain Williams.

There was plenty for the sisters to talk about and laugh over in their little sitting room upstairs. Their circle was widening. They were welcome guests at Manydown House, at Ibthorpe, and now at Rowling; Cassandra would be invited there frequently, most of all in times of crisis, because she had always been Edward's special sister. She would also be invited to stay at Kintbury with Fulwar and Eliza Fowle, and sometimes Tom Fowle would be staying there too. Their friendship continued quietly, without any fuss. Above all, Cassandra hated fuss.

Jane threw herself even more eagerly into all the excitement of balls and pretty dresses and the occasional flirtation. She was bewitching and she knew it. And if the steady, quiet understanding between Cassandra and Tom Fowle was going to grow into something which would eventually leave her out in the cold, then she must be armed against it in good time. Only she must not brood over it; nothing, surely, could ever separate her from Cassandra. "If Cassandra were going to have her head cut off," her

mother had said so often, "Jane would insist on sharing her fate."
How the joke had lingered on! And how ridiculously improbable
it had seemed. But people *did* get their heads cut off – nice people –
people Eliza de Feuillide had known, and danced with, and flirted
with, perhaps. It was as if a whole secure glittering world had suddenly been cracked to the core. During the early months of 1793
the news began to filter through that the king of France, Louis
XVI, had been tried and executed, and that the queen was likely to
share his fate. War was now inevitable and the young Austen brothers, Francis and Charles, were straining at the leash.

Jane was still writing. There was a kind of security there, in a
world of her own, however freely she shared it with Cassandra.
Some of the stories she wrote in that eventful year of 1792 were
curiously uneven. She would burst into delicious nonsense at one
moment and then the plot would tighten up and the characters
would develop a life of their own. Cassandra and the rest of the
family must have enjoyed a good laugh over the opening chapter
of *Leslie Castle*, when the wedding breakfast presented such a problem. Wedding breakfasts were surely an apt subject for anything
written in that particular year. Here the bridegroom is thrown
from his horse and fatally injured, just before the wedding day.
"Good God!" exclaims the bride's anxious sister; "you don't say
so? Why, what in the name of Heaven will become of all the Vic-
tuals?"

Leslie Castle is a story told in letters, uneven, lopsided, experi-
mental and eventually left unfinished. *Catherine*, which has a nonsensical dedication to Cassandra, represents a more sustained effort,
but eventually this story too was left unfinished. It was written
during the summer of 1792, at about the time when Jane Cooper
came to Steventon, before her marriage. Catherine is a young girl
brought up by a zealous maiden aunt, who watches over her conduct with "so scrutinizing a severity, as to make it very doubtful to

many people and to Catherine amongst the rest whether she loved her or not". Aunt is no caricature; she is the repressed, inhibited gentlewoman whose love for her ward can only be expressed in self-torturing suspicions of her conduct. Catherine would find refuge from her in a little bower in the garden where she and her friends used to play when they were small. The other little girls have left the village long since, but the bower still seems to comfort her with all its happy memories. One of her friends has suffered exactly the same fate as Eliza de Feuillide's mother, Philadelphia Austen; she has been shipped off to find a husband for herself in India. Catherine's indignant retort to one of her cousins who comments on this girl's good fortune may possibly convey the young Jane Austen's feelings in this matter. "Do you call it luck, for a girl of Genius and Feeling to be sent in quest of a Husband to Bengal to be married there to a Man of whose Disposition she has no opportunity of judging till her Judgment is of no use to her, who may be a Tyrant or a Fool or both for what she knows to the contrary. Do you call *that* fortunate?"

Young Catherine is alive to the tips of her fingers. So is her aunt, with all her psychological inhibitions, and so are all the other characters, the flighty, jealous cousin, the charming, teasing, flirtatious young man. This was no bright example of juvenile story-telling, with lifeless puppets to be manipulated at will; it was the opening of a mature novel which the immature author was not ready to complete. No wonder she laid it aside.

Some time during the next two years she wrote another story which must have disappointed her family, for there was not so much as a scrap of nonsense in it – "nothing to laugh at at all", as Mr and Mrs Ramsbottom found when they visited the seaside for the first time, or as Bob Hope said of *For Whom the Bell Tolls*, "there aren't many laughs in *that*". It was the story which had been gnawing like a rat at the back of her mind ever since she had heard

49

about the "wicked Mrs. Craven", which had gained impetus from her experience of heartless and ignorant snobbery, and which had put on the semblance of human flesh with her realization that evil natures do not necessarily show themselves in evil faces, that lovely women can be cruel, that handsome men can be fickle or treacherous, and that good, innocent people can be ensnared by the wicked. "Surely He shall deliver thee from the snare of the fowler," promised the Psalmist, but supposing – just supposing – that you did not see the snare, what then?

Jane called it *Lady Susan*, and when she had got it out of her system, she bundled the end of the story together light-heartedly. Many years later she was to make a fair copy of it and then put it away again. It was a theme she had no wish to pursue.

The members of the family had other things to think about. A new generation was coming into the world. James and Anne Austen had a little daughter, Anna, and in the more fashionable world Mr and Mrs Edward Austen announced the birth of their daughter, Fanny. Cassandra and Jane were now aunts, which seemed almost irresistibly funny to them, but from the first they were determined to be model aunts. Jane even dedicated a story to each infant. The ever-restless Henry was unsettled again. The general turmoil in Europe and the war with the new French Republic, which delighted the younger brothers, who saw in this the opportunity of a lifetime, made it impossible for him to enjoy life any longer in the cloistered atmosphere of Oxford. He had been on the point of making up his mind to take Orders, but in the present circumstances the prospect seemed unbearable. This was surely a time for action. He must be up and doing – precisely what, he did not know. At last he astonished the rest of the family by joining the Oxford Militia as an officer. The uniform suited his tall figure to perfection.

Eliza de Feuillide was anxiously awaiting news of her husband.

He must be all right, of course. He had been aware of some degree of danger when he left for France, but naturally he could not possibly risk losing his estates. Eliza had seen the sense of that; she could not have dissuaded him. Some of her friends were living quietly and nobody had arrested them or troubled them in any way. One of these was a charming lady called the Marquise de Marlboeuf.

Unlike many of the aristocracy, the Marquise de Marlboeuf knew how to manage her estates to advantage. In those difficult days, when everything was at sixes and sevens, you could not afford to waste good land or neglect sound farming practice. Some of the fields must harvest good grain, and some must grow hay and sanfoin for the cattle. There was to be no waste on the Marquise de Marlboeuf's estate; every acre must be used to advantage.

The accusation of the Committee of Public Safety came like a thunderbolt. The *ci-devant* Marquise was growing hay and sanfoin for her cattle in some of her fields, instead of wheat to feed the hungry people. Obviously she was allowing her land to run to waste with the aim of creating famine. She was an enemy of the people, and as such she must be brought to trial.

The Comte de Feuillide was horrified. The Marquise was one of his oldest friends. He flew to her rescue with thoughtless impetuosity. Never a highly intelligent man, he was rendered utterly stupid by panic. He could hardly rescue the Marquise bodily, and he recognized that any evidence he might offer would be disregarded. With what he believed to be supreme cunning, he decided to bribe the witnesses. After all, he still had plenty of money. They took the bribes delightedly and he sighed with relief. The danger was over and the Marquise de Marlboeuf could return to her home in the country, or emigrate to England and stay with Eliza for a while until he could join them both. How delightful it would be! Unfortunately, the witnesses felt it their duty to take his money and then denounce him to the Committee of Public Safety for bribing them, and trying to interfere with the cause of justice. It was a shocking crime in the eyes of the Committee of Public Safety, and the Comte was summarily arrested. A mockery of a trial followed and both he and the Marquise de Marlboeuf were sentenced to death.

On 12 February, 1794, the Marquise de Marlboeuf and the Comte de Feuillide were driven through the narrow streets of Paris in a tumbril, with the shouts of the mob ringing in their ears, to perish under the sharp knife of the guillotine. Little Hastings would never see his kind *papa* come riding home again.

5

IT MUST HAVE seemed to those who experienced it like living in two worlds: one where everything seemed to have fallen to pieces, and the other which still jogged along in the same old way. At one time many people in England had been excited by the new ideas in France, by the overthrow of despotic power and the proclaiming of Liberty, Equality and Fraternity. Now the admirers of the new regime were drawing back, repelled by the horrible excesses of the mob and the slaughter of innocent people. The advance of new ideas and ideals was set back in England for almost a generation by the events on the other side of the Channel.

Life at the parsonage in Steventon may have seemed remote from these happenings, yet the family had been directly touched by them. When Eliza de Feuillide came to stay, wearing her mourning dress, with her delicate little son at her side, they could not help being reminded of that blood-stained scaffold where her husband had met his death. But Eliza was not suited to a tragic role. She might well have echoed Dr Johnson's friend, Oliver Edwards: "I have tried too in my time to be a philosopher; but, I don't know how, cheerfulness kept breaking in." Certainly it was not very long before cheerfulness seemed to be breaking in, and Eliza became even more enchanting than before, with the touch of romantic pathos belonging to her sad story. Jane as a little girl had almost worshipped her cousin, and there would always be a warm friendship between them, but now it seemed as if the adoring child had suddenly grown up and the rose-coloured spectacles had been removed. Like Eliza, Jane was charming, witty and attractive; she loved dancing and chatter and fun; but Jane was also, in a quiet way, becoming a pretty shrewd judge of people, including Eliza.

A year after the Comte de Feuillide's execution, there was another death in the family circle. James's delicate wife died after a long time of ill health; she had recovered but slowly after the birth of her baby, Anna, and the hard winter of 1794/5 was too much for her. She struggled through it painfully, but died in the following spring. James was heartbroken; he could not bear to hear little Anna asking for her mother, so he sent the child to Steventon to be cared for by his mother and sisters. Cassandra and Jane were delighted, and Anna soon settled down with them. It was not long before she discovered that Aunt Jane could tell fascinating stories, even to a baby niece who might have been considered too young to profit by this attention. There was something about Aunt Jane's voice that held the little thing spellbound.

It was during this summer of 1795 that Cassandra became engaged to Tom Fowle. Cassandra still insisted that there must be no fuss. Their boy and girl friendship had slipped naturally into this closer relationship but talk of marriage in the near future seemed premature. The prospects of the young couple depended entirely upon a wealthy young relation of the bridegroom's, Lord Craven; he was very friendly with his cousin Tom, and was confidently expected to present him with a living in due course. A number of good livings were at his disposal and the most likely one to fall vacant in the near future was in Shropshire. This would be the very thing for Tom Fowle. Mrs Austen regarded the presentation as a foregone conclusion, and spoke of the time which was coming before long when Cassandra would be "gone into Shropshire and

Jane the Lord knows where".

With Jane it was certainly a case of "the Lord knows where". Young men seemed to find her irresistible. Some were warned off by zealous mammas, anxious for their sons to marry money, and well aware that the Austens, despite their good connections, had nothing to bestow upon their pretty daughters; some were discomfited by Jane's witty tongue; others, like the schoolboy brother of Elizabeth, Catherine and Alethea Bigg, sighed after her at too young an age and were ridiculed or disregarded; but there were still plenty of attractive young men to partner her at dances and balls, and engage in sparkling conversation.

One of Jane's friendships attracted a good deal of attention and Cassandra, who so hated any kind of fuss, became alarmed. The young man in question was Tom Lefroy, nephew of the Reverend Isaac Lefroy of Ashe, whose charming wife, Madame Lefroy, had long been Jane's older friend and confidante. Surely there could be nothing in it if Madame Lefroy allowed and encouraged the friendship? Tom was an Irishman, young and handsome and debonair; he danced to perfection and his quiet wit enabled him to give as good as he got in repartee. Mrs Lefroy enjoyed seeing the young people so happy together; of course there was nothing more to it than that.

Tom Lefroy was a brilliant young man, and his friends in Ireland prophesied a great future for him. He would go far if only he could be encouraged to meet the right people, and seize the right opportunities, and make the right kind of marriage. He could flirt with anybody he liked, provided he settled down eventually and married a girl with some money behind her. Meanwhile it was good for him to visit his English relations, and enjoy the balls and dances of a country neighbourhood, and doubtless break hearts by the dozen.

At some point Madame Lefroy must have taken the alarm.

Probably it was at much the same time that Cassandra became anxious for her sister. She might hate "fuss" for herself, but any kind of gossip about Jane must have been almost unbearable, and it seemed obvious that there had been a good deal of talk amongst those who had watched the behaviour of the young people at a ball given by the Harwoods at Deane House. Cassandra was staying with Fulwar and Eliza Fowle at Kintbury, too far away to intervene, but she wrote Jane a sisterly letter which must have stung her to the quick.

Jane replied very promptly, putting up such an effective smoke-screen that nobody to this day has professed to know for certain what her feelings actually were.

'You scold me so much in the nice long letter which I have this moment received from you, that I am almost afraid to tell you how my Irish friend and I behaved. Imagine to yourself everything most profligate and shocking in the way of dancing and sitting down together. I *can* expose myself, however, only *once more*, because he leaves the country soon after next Friday, on which day we *are* to have a dance at Ashe after all. He is a very gentleman-like, good-looking, pleasant young man, I assure you. But as to our having met, except at the last three balls, I cannot say much; for he is so excessively laughed at about me at Ashe, that he is ashamed of coming to Steventon, and ran away when we called on Mrs. Lefroy a few days ago.'

Later in this same letter, she adds that Tom Lefroy and his cousin George have just paid an unexpected call at the Parsonage. "He has but *one* fault," she observed, "which he will, I trust, entirely remove – it is that his morning coat is a great deal too light."

In her next letter to Cassandra, written just before the ball at Ashe, Jane admits that she rather expects "to receive an offer from my friend in the course of the evening. I shall refuse him, however, unless he promises to give away his white coat." Whether the offer is to be made or not, she maintains her smoke-screen of indifference and assures her sister that she does not care sixpence for him. In a continuation of the letter on the following day, she comments: "At length the day is come on which I am to flirt my last with Tom Lefroy, and when you receive this it will be over."

Long afterwards, when Cassandra was an elderly lady, she destroyed any of Jane's letters, or parts of them, which she felt were too revealing, but these paragraphs were left untouched. The smoke-screen must have been effective. Even Cassandra cannot have known the truth of the matter. It was left to a very distinguished gentleman, the Lord Chief Justice of Ireland, to confess to his nephew, who had asked him about Jane Austen, that he had been in love with her, although he qualified his confession by saying that it was a boyish love.

Jane herself probably never revealed the true story, even to Cassandra. Nevertheless, she must have reached some kind of understanding with her sister, for a couple of years later, when Cassandra was staying with Edward and Elizabeth at Godmersham, she mentioned in one of her letters an encounter with Mrs Lefroy: "Mrs. Lefroy did come last Wednesday, and the Harwoods came likewise, but very considerately paid their visit before Mrs. Lefroy's arrival, with whom, in spite of interruptions both from my father and James, I was enough alone to hear all that was interesting which you will easily credit when I tell you that of her nephew she said nothing at all, and of her friend very little. She did not once mention the name of the former to *me*, and I was too proud to make any enquiry, but on my father's afterwards asking where he was, I learnt that he was gone back to London and on his way to Ireland, where he is called to the Bar and means to practice."

Mrs Lefroy was a little more communicative about her "friend", a Fellow of Emmanuel College called Samuel Blackall, who had been staying at Ashe with the Lefroys. He had found Jane very attractive, but his financial position would not allow him to pursue the interest he undoubtedly felt. Here Jane was believed to be heart-whole, and she probably was, but not to such an extent that she could contemplate his marriage many years later with any great satisfaction. In a long letter written to Francis at sea, she wrote:

> I wonder whether you happened to see Mr Blackall's marriage in the Papers last Jany. *We* did. He was married at Clifton to a Miss Lewis, whose father had been late of Antigua. I should very much like to know what sort of a Woman she is. He was a piece of Perfection, noisy Perfection himself which I always recollect with regard. – we had noticed a few months before his succeeding to a College Living, the very Living which we remember his talking of & wishing for; an exceeding good one, Great Cadbury in Somersetshire. – I would wish Miss Lewis to be of a silent turn & rather ignorant, but naturally intelligent & wishing to learn; – fond of cold veal pies, green tea in the afternoon, & a green window blind at night.

Mr Blackall would never have done, of course; if he had possessed all the gold in Ethiopia, he would never have done. All the same, she could not bring herself to wish for him a paragon of a wife.

Jane never forgot what it felt like to be a young girl in love. Those moments touched with magic would live on in her memory; the soft Irish voice, whispering in her ear; the touch of his hand on hers as they threaded their way through one of the "country dances" popular at the time; the lilt of shared laughter as they found that they laughed at the same jokes. Nobody would ever spoil it for her. Nobody could do that, not even Cassandra. Only the pain which came afterwards would always be there too; it was the price she had to pay and she would never know that he had had to pay it too.

Jane was still writing. This time it was another story told in letters; somehow it felt more impersonal that way, but she was not really satisfied with it. It was about three sisters, Elinor, Marianne and Margaret, but Margaret did not seem to matter very much, except as the writer or recipient of some of the letters, so she called the story *Elinor and Marianne*. She must have shared it with Cassandra, and later with the rest of the family, but possibly this time there may not have been quite the same spontaneity about the sharing of her story. Families are often a little apt to jump to conclusions, and identify characters, and on a superficial judgement it would have been easy to identify Elinor, the sensible, disciplined sister, with Cassandra, and the lovely, uncontrolled Marianne, all romance and sensibility, with Jane. Such an identification would have been quite mistaken, of course, but in any case nothing can be known for certain about this early version of the story, for it was soon re-cast in narrative form and the original manuscript destroyed. The new version had a fresh title: *Sense and Sensibility*.

Before re-writing *Elinor and Marianne* however, Jane had embarked upon an entirely new story. At first this was kept secret from the rest of the family, except for Cassandra and one small listener, playing on the floor at their feet. Little Anna was far too small, they thought, to pay any attention to what was going on. But little Anna was an unusually intelligent child, and when her young aunts went off into peals of laughter, she naturally tried to make out what it was all about. She caught the names of some of the characters and began to repeat them in the parlour downstairs, until lovingly silenced by Cassandra and Jane. "It's a secret!" they explained, and little Anna nodded importantly. They might think she was only a baby, but she would show that she could be trusted with a grown-up secret.

The relationship with the two sisters was now, if anything, closer than ever. Tom Lefroy had ridden away, out of Jane's life and into a wider world which would make or break him; Tom Fowle, ever constant in his devotion to Cassandra, had left for the West Indies as chaplain to Lord Craven's regiment. It was an excellent opportunity for the young man and the experience would stand him in good stead later on. Cassandra, with two brothers in the navy, was used to long separations; she stitched away at her wedding clothes as she listened appreciatively to Jane's latest nonsensical creation. For Jane, this resumption of the old relationship must have brought a respite. Some day Tom Fowle would return; some day he and Cassandra would be married and go to that desirable living in Shropshire, and raise a tribe of children in the parsonage. Never for a moment would Jane have to admit that she felt left out. She would doubtless be the unmarried daughter left at home to look after her parents; the maiden aunt to be depended on by the rest of the family; but when her parents were gone, what then? It does not do to look too far ahead, of course, but Jane had an unusually vivid imagination. Perhaps this partly explains her sensitive understanding of impecunious ladies later on.

The girls' shabby little sitting room· was a scene of almost constant activity, except when one or other of the sisters was away, which did not happen often. As Edward and Elizabeth's family rapidly increased, Cassandra, Edward's special sister, was often needed at Rowling, but during the summer of 1796 Jane paid a long visit there with Frank. They travelled by way of

London, where they stayed in a hotel in Cork Street, Piccadilly, and went to Astley's circus, which was one of the most popular entertainments in town. At Rowling they met Henry, handsome, restless, and brilliant as ever, who appeared to be fascinated by a Miss Pearson. Jane was not at all sure about the young lady, and when it was suggested that Henry might convey her home, bringing also Miss Pearson to stay with his mother and sisters, Jane wrote hurriedly to Cassandra, warning her not to expect too much beauty. "I will not pretend to say that on *first veiw* she quite answered the opinion I had formed of her; – my mother I am sure will be disappointed if she does not take great care." However, the plan fell through, as did most of the plans for her return journey. In those days, young ladies did not travel alone. In one of her letters she suggested that her father might come for her. "My father will be so good as to fetch home his prodigal Daughter from Town, I hope, unless he wishes me to walk the Hospitals, Enter at the Temple, or mount guard at St. James. It will hardly be in Frank's power to take me home." The three suggestions in the letter must have seemed utterly ridiculous at the time, and just the kind of nonsensical thing that Jane would suggest. Nowadays, only the third would be impossible for a woman.

Frank had been thoroughly enjoying himself at Rowling. He went out shooting with Edward, while indoors he tried his hand at wood-turning and made a capital little butter churn for Fanny to play with. Fanny was now three years old and she had two little brothers: Edward, who had just been breeched – "and whipped into the bargain", said Jane in a letter to Cassandra – and the new baby, George, whom Jane was allowed to hold in her arms for a few minutes, "which I thought very kind". Frank and Jane also went to dances together, and Jane had the honour of opening the ball at Goodneston, her sister-in-law's former home, with Elizabeth's brother, Edward Bridges, the young master of the house. Jane's experience was widening. She would always take pride in being a provincial, and her ideal would always be life in a village or a little country town, but Edward's new relations brought her into close touch with people in more aristocratic circles and she was not slow to observe their ways.

The problem of Jane's return to Steventon was eventually solved, though not without further complications. Frank, who had been depended on as escort, received his sailing orders for the frigate *Triton*; Henry was unwell and Miss Pearson elusive. At one point Jane complained to Cassandra that she was "just like Camilla in Mr. Dubster's summerhouse, for my Lionel will have taken away my ladder by which I came here; or at least by which I intended to get away". This was a reference to Fanny Burney's latest novel, *Camilla*, which had been published that year. Jane had subscribed for the five volumes, doubtless at her father's expense, and the whole family had enjoyed them. Another problem troubled Jane at Rowling, and she wrote off to Cassandra for advice. She knew she ought to tip Richis, one of the maidservants who had been helpful to her, but how much ought she to give? Should it be a guinea? Or could she offer five shillings? Staying with wealthy relations might be very enjoyable, but it involved the guests in difficulties which their hosts could not possibly be expected to understand. The difference between five shillings and a guinea was a mere nothing to Edward and Elizabeth.

Once Jane Austen had settled in comfortably at Steventon again, the old routine was resumed, with the household tasks, and the visits to neighbours and poor parishioners, and the many hours spent in writing at her desk in the little sitting room upstairs and reading the results aloud to Cassandra, with little Anna playing happily at their feet. Only it did not look as if Anna would be with them much longer. It seemed very likely that she would soon have a stepmother and return to the rectory at Deane.

From a very early stage it had seemed likely that James would marry again. He had been utterly inconsolable at the time of Anne's death, unable to settle down, and unable to comfort even his little daughter. At one time, people thought he might marry Eliza de Feuillide. Certainly she flirted with him outrageously, but then she had always been an incorrigible flirt. Only it was said that she could not bear to contemplate marrying a clergyman and James was a clergyman to his fingertips. On the other hand, he seemed infatuated by Eliza. Certainly she seemed to take a frivolous view of life, but most of that could be laid at the door of her upbringing. The Reverend George Austen had always been suspicious of the result of educating a young girl in Paris, however much he might dote on his pretty niece. Tradition says that James did indeed propose, but was rejected on account of his calling. It was not long before Eliza was flirting again with her handsome cousin Henry, let alone a horde of other possible suitors. Meanwhile, James turned his attentions elsewhere. There were two eligible young ladies, both called Mary, and in the end Mary Lloyd was the chosen one. Eliza de Feuillide could not help being a little waspish on the subject. She wrote to Philadelphia Walter that Mary was not "rich or handsome", but added that she was "very sensible and good-humoured". The charming Eliza may have had her faults, but she seldom failed to show a generous spirit. Mrs Austen was delighted with the engagement. She had never cared much for Eliza, whereas Mary Lloyd was a young lady after her own heart. "You, my dear Mary," she wrote, "are the very person I should have chosen for James's wife, Anna's mother and my daughter."

James and Mary were married in January, 1797, and little Anna was able to return to her own home. It was a pity that she never really took to her stepmother. She had only the faintest remembrance of her own mother as "a tall and slender lady dressed in white", but she resented the intruder in a way that nobody had expected. After all, the child knew Martha and Mary Lloyd perfectly well; they were her aunts' friends and her grandmother's favourites. Only nobody had suggested that someday she might have to call Mary "mama".

The winter passed and spring followed, and now and then letters would come from dear Tom Fowle, far away in the West Indies. They would come in batches, as the ships came into port, and Cassandra, longing for news, would read them first hurriedly, then slowly, and then over and over again till the next batch came. It was a long time to wait, but many other girls were in the same position, some of them with lovers engaged in various expeditions against the French, in which they might even be killed and never come home again. After all, Tom was not a soldier or a sailor. There was no likelihood of his being killed.

When the ocean was stormy, there would be no letter for a long time. The girls would remind one another of the Atlantic gales, and the little ships battling their way homewards or running for shelter in some island harbour. It was no use fretting if there was no news. No news was better than bad news. When the bad news did come, nobody could believe it. This thing could not have happened – this awful, unimaginable thing. It could not be true that all the time they were comforting one another with tales of ships delayed by storm and tempest, Tom Fowle, kind, gentle, uncomplaining Tom had been lying in his grave at San Domingo. Tom Fowle, Cassandra's "dear and only love", had died out there in February, of the yellow fever.

Cassandra laid aside her wedding clothes. Her busy needle would never stitch at them again. Afterwards Lord Craven swore that if he had known about the engagement, he would never have let young Tom go out to such an unhealthy place. Young men were two a penny, so it seemed, but if he had known – if only somebody had told him – if only – if only –. It would have needed only that to break Cassandra's gentle heart, if it had not been broken already.

6

THERE MUST HAVE been something therapeutic about all the writing and the reading aloud that went on in the little sitting room upstairs during the summer months of 1797. Cassandra was not one to indulge in self-pity, or to expect unending consolation and sympathy from others. Jane's imaginary world was good to live in at a time when she needed some kind of barrier against the obtrusive, well-meaning, but exquisitely painful attentions of the world outside. The revision of *Elinor and Marianne*, under its new title, *Sense and Sensibility*, went on apace. The other, newer story was finished in August; it had a title now, *First Impressions*. When at last the secret was revealed and other members of the family were able to enjoy it, there was almost a sensation. This was the best thing Jane had written. More than that, it was actually a *book* – a real novel. They did not hesitate to compare it with Fanny Burney's *Evelina*.

First Impressions had been read and re-read by the family many times before the Reverend George Austen decided to take an important step. If this novel was as good as Fanny Burney's *Evelina*, then surely it ought to be published. Unfortunately he did not know how one set about approaching a publisher. Eventually he made up his mind. He wrote to a good London publishing firm, Messrs Cadell, telling them that he had in his possession "a manuscript Novel, comprising three volumes, about the length of Miss Burney's *Evelina*," and suggested that if they thought well of the novel, it could be published at the author's expense – which of course meant at his expense, but he probably thought it might be impolitic to say so. Admittedly, Fanny Burney had been very young when she wrote *Evelina*, but possibly the publishers might be more favourably disposed to a mature author. "Should you give any encouragement, I will send you the work," he wrote at the end of the letter.

Messrs Cadell gave no encouragement. They must have received many letters from fond relations of budding authors, and they were only thankful that the actual manuscript had not been sent. They filed away the letter in case this credulous country clergyman wrote again and that, they thought, was the end of the matter. It was not. The manuscript which they refused even to read was an early version of what was to prove a masterpiece: *Pride and Prejudice*. And there was to be a curious sequel to the affair. When, many years later, Cadells went out of business and their effects were disposed of, the Reverend George Austen's letter came out of its file to be sold with everything else. It was bought by an Irish gentleman called Thomas Lefroy.

Soon after the rejection of *First Impressions*, Cassandra and Jane paid a visit to Bath with their mother. Their mother's brother, James Leigh Perrot and his wife lived there during the winter months at a rather gloomy house, Number 1 Paragon. During the summer they lived at their country house, called Scarlets, in Berkshire. It is possible that Cassandra and Jane thought of Number 1 Paragon and of Bath itself as a gloomy place because their visits there had never been particularly happy ones. The Leigh Perrots were a wealthy, childless couple, very wrapped up in each other and not used to the company of young people. It must have been impressed on the Austen children from an early age that they should on no account upset their uncle and aunt. James was considered to be Mr Leigh Perrot's heir, so he would in due course inherit a quite considerable fortune. Whether Mrs Austen thought that her brother might possibly do something for the girls is not known; he would certainly have been in a position to do so, had he so wished or had his wife approved.

The girls were very fond of their uncle, who was kind to them and often gave them pocket money to spend in the shops. He liked to take his pretty nieces about the place and to see them coming back excitedly with their purchases. Their aunt was another matter. She did not understand children and young people, or even like them particularly, and her manner to them was forbidding. Thus there was a shadow over Bath and especially over Number 1 Paragon. A child can grow up with an impression of a place which may completely belie its real character, like the young mother who would not take her children to a popular Welsh seaside resort "because it was so dark there". It was nothing of the kind, but she had been unhappy there as a little child.

Probably when the first excitement was over and the Bath shops fully explored, the girls longed to be back at Steventon again, but journeys in those days were such complicated affairs that nobody would think of paying a short visit anywhere. It was a full month before they returned, to find that brilliant, wayward, restless Henry had captured the heart of his equally restless but charming cousin, Eliza de Feuillide, ten years his senior. They were married quietly in London on 31 December at St Marylebone Church and not one of their relations attended the wedding. It hardly seemed an auspicious beginning, but the marriage was to be one of unbroken happiness, except for the grief caused by the early death of little Hastings de Feuillide in 1801. He had always been a delicate child, subject to fits and unlikely to grow to maturity, but throughout his short life he enjoyed the love and care of a devoted mother and, latterly, of a kind stepfather.

Far from being depressed by the rejection unread of *First Impressions*, Jane had embarked on another story. Possibly her recent visit to Bath may have sparked it off, for it was all about a very young girl visiting Bath for the first time. Like Cassandra and Jane, she was a parson's daughter and one of a large family and, like them, she was a great reader of romantic novels. Unlike them, however, she believed every word she read and set off on her adventures expecting to meet handsome heroes, sinister villains, distressed damsels, ruined castles, starving prisoners, and dismal oubliettes at every turn. The story still has the dew on it – possibly because for a curious reason, Jane never had a chance to revise it as thoroughly as she could have wished. She called it *Susan*, which may well prove that she never intended to take *Lady Susan* off the shelf. The little heroine's name was Susan, but years later Jane changed it to Catherine. The hero was a delightful young gentleman called Henry Tilney, and there are critics today who say that of all Jane Austen's characters, he is the one who most resembles his creator, which may possibly indicate that she had her favourite brother, Henry, in mind, for brother and sister were said by some to be like one another in many ways.

Susan was a light-hearted book. Jane endowed her dear little goose of a heroine with two of the most sensible parents she ever depicted, and so there could be no doubt that, in spite of all her romantic nonsense and the silly mistakes she made, she would come to no harm. Indeed, she would eventually acquire an eminently sensible husband in Henry Tilney, as sensible as her own father, and a member of the same profession. There was laughter again in the little sitting room upstairs, as Jane read page after page of the new story to Cassandra.

The summer brought sudden tragedy. Their cousin, Jane Cooper, who had been so happily married to Captain Williams of the Royal Navy, was killed in a carriage accident. So far as could be ascertained, it had been nobody's fault. Jane had been bowling happily along in a one-horse chaise, when suddenly a frightened dray-horse had bolted into the road and crashed into the vehicle. She had been thrown out and killed instantly. It was a terrible shock for Cassandra and Jane. They had always liked their cousin, ever since they had all been at school together, and she had refused to be browbeaten by the formidable Mrs Cawley. If it had not been for Jane Cooper, what would have become of them?

Some time afterwards, Mr and Mrs Austen and their daughters set off for Godmersham in Kent. This was a very special visit, for it was their first since Edward and Elizabeth and their children had moved into the great mansion where Edward had lived with his adoptive parents before his marriage. Rowling had been a very pleasant home and he had been very happy there, but the widowed Mrs Knight had decided, four years after her husband's death, to hand over the whole property to Edward and retire to a much smaller house, White Friars, near Canterbury. Another great house went with the property, Chawton House, near Alton in Hampshire, but for the time being Edward and Elizabeth pre-ferred to live at Godmersham, especially as it was in comparatively easy reach of Canterbury and also of Goodneston, where Elizabeth's parents lived. Godmersham was a beautiful, stately mansion, set in a great deer park, in pretty undulating country watered by the river Stour. Edward and Elizabeth were an ideal host and hostess, and their growing family of children provided a constant source of interest and delight. Little Fanny was growing into a fascinating child, pretty and affectionate, but Jane's favour-ite at this stage was the little boy she had been allowed to hold in her arms two years before, when he was a baby. Little George – or "Itty Dordy" as he called himself – continued to be a pet of hers for some time, though she did not flatter herself by thinking that their special relationship would continue. Sweet-natured, affectionate little boys have a habit of growing up into "ungovernable, ungracious fellows", she thought, but meanwhile she would enjoy this stage while it lasted.

Jane and her parents left Godmersham in October, but Cassandra stayed behind. Elizabeth had recently given birth to her fifth child and fourth son, William, and her sister-in-law's help was really needed. There was indeed the dependable and dearly loved children's nurse, Sackree, and a host of devoted servants, but nobody could quite take the place of Cassandra.

The journey home was not without its trials and vexations, though it began auspiciously enough. The travellers took it in stages, driving first to Sittingbourne, which they left in a very heavy shower. It was not long before the clouds cleared away and, as Jane described it in a letter to Cassandra, "we had a very bright *chrystal* afternoon". The description evokes the aftermath of a heavy shower so clearly that one can almost catch the smell of damp earth after heavy rain.

The party went on to Rochester and then to Dartford, where they spent the night. Soon after their arrival, Jane discovered that her writing and dressing boxes had been put into somebody else's chaise, which was just being loaded with luggage as they drove in. In the confusion, the luggage had been mixed up, and by the time Jane discovered her loss, the writing and dressing boxes were being whisked off to Gravesend by a traveller who was going to the West Indies. This was a serious matter for Jane. The writing box contained all the money she possessed, amounting to seven pounds. It might also have been a serious matter for posterity, for it probably contained some of her manuscripts. Fortunately the discovery was made in time for a horseman to be dispatched after the chaise; he caught up with the traveller after about two or three miles and retrieved the missing boxes. Doubtless they were able to enjoy their five o'clock dinner with a better appetite as a result. They had "some beef steaks and a boiled fowl," Jane wrote to Cassandra, "but no oyster sauce". Possibly oyster sauce was served with the boiled fowl at Godmersham.

So far Mrs Austen had stood the journey well, but next day she was tired out by the time they reached Staines, where they spent the night. Jane was thankful next day when they reached Basingstoke, where they rested for half an hour before going on to Steventon. The local apothecary recommended twelve drops of laudanum, to compose Mrs Austen's nerves, and Jane felt very responsible as she measured it out exactly, for this duty would normally have been undertaken by Cassandra. She wrote to her sister with detailed accounts of every stage of the journey and then continued with local news and gossip. Naturally she had no idea that anybody else would read the letter, or that critics two hundred years later would pick out a certain passage and accuse her of being callous or heartless. "Mrs. Hall of Sherborne was brought to bed yesterday of a dead child, some days before she expected it, owing to a fright," wrote Jane. "I suppose she happened unawares to look at her husband." Obviously Mr Hall's unprepossessing countenance must have been a joke between the sisters for some time; if there had been anything more to it than that, Cassandra would have cut out the passage when she "censored" Jane's letters long after her sister's death. Miscarriages and dead births were all too frequent in those days, when for the most part a "gap" between children in a family implied that an infant had been miscarried.

Jane enjoyed being in charge of the housekeeping at the parsonage. Her mother told her to tell Cassandra that she was "a very good housekeeper", and she passed on the comment with pride, adding that she thought it was her "peculiar excellence, and for this reason – I always take care to provide such things as please my own appetite, which I consider as the chief merit in housekeeping". She and her parents enjoyed ragout veal one day and haricot mutton the next, and Jane was planning to have an ox cheek soon with dumplings. The mutton would probably be from one of their own Leicestershire sheep, in which her father took great pride.

James and Mary were now expecting their first child. Mary had suffered a bad miscarriage previously, and now she was in the last stage of pregnancy, longing for all to be safely over. Everybody was inclined to be nervous, especially as two of the neighbours had died quite recently in childbirth. The family agreed that Mary must on no account hear of this, and Mrs Austen became so nervous that she asked to be told nothing until all was over and the baby was born. Mercifully all went happily and well, and little James Edward Austen – to be known as Edward – came safely into the world, to the delight of all concerned. When Jane first saw him he was asleep, but she was assured that his eyes were large, dark and handsome.

Jane was inclined to be critical of Mary; they had been friends for many years, but the eldest of the Lloyd sisters, Martha, had always been her favourite. "Mary does not manage such things in such a way as to make me want to lay in myself," she wrote to Cassandra. "She is not tidy enough in her appearance; she has no dressing gown to sit up in; her curtains are all too thin, and things are not in that comfort and style about her which are necessary to make such a situation an enviable one. Elizabeth was really a pretty object with her nice clean cap put on so tidily and her dress so uniformly white and orderly." It was all very well for Elizabeth, of course, she had a very wealthy husband and a host of efficient servants.

Cassandra's visit seemed to be dragging on, doubtless delightfully for her, but for Jane the novelty of housekeeping by herself had lost some of its glamour. She wrote long letters to Cassandra with all the local news. Mrs Martin had opened a circulating library, and Mrs Austen had offered to pay the subscription on behalf of her daughters. Jane took exception to Mrs Martin's introductory letter. "Mrs. Martin tells us that her Collection is not to consist only of novels, but of every kind of Literature, etc, etc. – She might have spared this pretension to *our* family, who are great Novel-readers and not ashamed of being so; – but it was necessary, I suppose to the self-consequence of half her Subscribers." This sentiment was to find its way into *Susan*, (later *Northanger Abbey*), where Jane accuses readers of "decrying the capacity and undervaluing the labour of the novelist, and of slighting the performances which have only genius, wit and taste to recommend them". Later on poor Mrs Martin's business failed and Jane expressed great sympathy with her in her difficulties.

Jane also wrote to Cassandra about the local balls and dances, but these could not compete with Godmersham and Goodneston, though Jane made a hit at one of them, when she borrowed a frill from Cassandra's black bonnet and contrived an enchanting black cap, with a length of silver ribbon bound round it and a startling red feather. Jane loved dancing as much as ever, though she tended to have trouble with her eyes afterwards, because of the dust. Obviously Cassandra was going to much grander balls and Jane could not help envying her a little; she had gone to one at Ashford which was attended by Prince William of Gloucester. Twice she mentioned in her letter how glad she was that Cassandra had danced at Ashford and "supped with the Prince"; perhaps Cassandra may have been tempted to comment "the lady doth protest too much, methinks".

Both sisters were eager for news of their sailor brothers. These were stirring times in the navy; the Battle of the Nile had been fought earlier that year and the victory had been celebrated in every town in the country. No young officer wanted to remain in obscurity when his profession offered such opportunities for glory, let alone for making a fortune. "Frank is made," wrote Jane hurriedly to Cassandra. "He was yesterday raised to the Rank of Commander and appointed to the *Petterel* Sloop now at Gibraltar." Their "own particular little brother" had become so impatient with the delay in promotion that his father had made an application to Admiral Gambier on his behalf, and he was now to be removed to the *Tamar* frigate. He came to visit his parents before leaving and impressed all their friends by his good looks and dashing appearance. He wore his hair cropped and unpowdered, a style of which his brother, Edward, did not at all approve. Edward, now an affluent country gentleman and a considerable landowner, was rapidly becoming conventional in outlook. He was also inclined to be fussy about his health, unlike his impecunious sisters, who could enjoy cross-country walks or dance into the small hours and be none the worse for it. Jane was a loving sister and a devoted daughter; it was only in confidence to Cassandra that she sometimes betrayed a little impatience with people who became preoccupied with their own state of health. Mrs Austen, now that her children were all grown up and, like Othello, with her "occupation gone", tended to dwell on her ailments. "She would tell you herself that she has a very dreadful cold in her head at present," wrote Jane to Cassandra. "But I have not much compassion for colds in the head without fever or sore throat."

Edward's recent preoccupation with his health turned out in the end to be very much to Jane's advantage, for eventually he decided to take the waters at Bath, in the hope of relieving his gout. He was to be accompanied by Elizabeth and the older children, Fanny and Edward, and also by his mother and Jane. Jane was delighted at the prospect of a visit to Bath which did not involve staying with the Leigh Perrots, and Cassandra was glad to settle down again at home and look after her father. Jane wrote to Cassandra in high spirits after the journey. They had stayed at Devizes on the way, and Edward had ordered a delicious meal for them, with amongst other things a dish of asparagus and a lobster – how Cassandra would have enjoyed it! – and cheese cakes as a treat for the children. The house where they stayed in Bath was to everybody's liking, with large, well-furnished rooms, an agreeable landlady and – to the children's great joy – a little black kitten frisking about on the staircase. Jane was delighted with everything and sent back lively accounts to Cassandra of her shopping expeditions, and the Bath fashions, and all the people she met. Some of the sisterly jokes, which naturally were never intended for public consumption, caused raised eyebrows amongst the critics who read them long after both sisters were gone. How could Jane refer to Dr Hall in such an unfeeling way? – "Dr. Hall in such very deep mourning that either his mother, or his wife, or himself must be dead." If Jane had written her letters to Cassandra with only future critics in mind, they would doubtless have made much duller reading.

Jane was kept busy shopping for various members of the family, but she wanted to draw the line at buying shoes for Martha. It was difficult to buy shoes for other people and they were such awkward things to pack. She astonished Cassandra with her account of the fashionable hats; people in Bath were wearing, not only artificial flowers, but fruit in their hats. Jane was tempted at first, but the bunches of artificial fruit were very expensive, even at the cheap milliner's shop which her aunt had recommended, and eventually she decided perforce that it was "more natural to have flowers grow out of the head than fruit". Aunt Leigh Perrot was very helpful over the shopping; she seemed to be much more interested in her relations when they were not actually staying in her house. The feeling was mutual; even Number 1 Paragon seemed a brighter place to Jane when she was not sleeping under its somewhat inhospitable roof.

Fanny and Edward enjoyed their holiday with gusto, though doubtless nothing quite came up to those cheese cakes at Devizes. They sent messages to their grandfather and Cassandra, and to James and Mary and Anna and the baby; little Edward widened the circle with tender enquiries after the turkeys and the ducks and the chickens. He also informed his Aunt Cassandra that he and Fanny liked gooseberry pie and gooseberry pudding very much, and it is to be hoped that Cassandra remembered this when the children stayed at Steventon on their way home. One thing seemed to puzzle the observant Fanny; when Aunt Cassandra wrote to them, the wafers fastening down the little notes were quite damp, as if they had only just been put on, whereas she would have expected them to be dry after their long journey by post. Clever as she was, she never suspected that they had come enclosed in Cassandra's letter to Jane, and that Jane had carefully put on the wafers to make them look as if they had come through the mail. She would go to any amount of trouble for a child.

The little sitting room at the parsonage seemed a long way away, and so did that other world which she loved to share with her sister. Nevertheless, Jane flared up in mock alarm when Martha sent a message asking if she might re-read *First Impressions*. Jane would not hear of it. "She means to publish it from memory," she wrote jokingly, "and one more perusal must enable her to do it." This was nonsense, of course, and both the sisters knew it. What Cassandra probably did not know was that *First Impressions* was part of Jane's very self and not to be touched lightly even by Martha, who was one of her dearest friends.

"I am very happy at Bath," wrote little Fanny to her Aunt Cassandra, and doubtless every other member of the family party would have said the same. The child added that Papa did not seem very much better for drinking the waters; nevertheless, his spirits must have revived considerably, for he bought a pair of black coach horses for sixty guineas and seemed very pleased with his purchase. Altogether the holiday had been a great success, even for Jane, who had always tended to dislike Bath, and for the Leigh Perrots, who had always seemed so set in their ways. They may even have felt some regret when the big party of Austens, old and young, rumbled away in their carriages, though doubtless it was a relief to return to their old routine again. Unfortunately, the old routine did not last long for the Leigh Perrots. Jane and her mother returned to Steventon in June, and the Edward Austens, after a stay at the parsonage, went on to Godmersham. In August came the shocking news that Aunt Leigh Perrot had been arrested and accused of shop-lifting. It was fantastic; it was incredible; her relations did not believe a word of it.

The story was an all too common one. Mrs Leigh Perrot, that clever and experienced shopper, who always had an eye for a good bargain, went to a little milliner's shop at the corner of Bath Street. It was not a particularly fashionable shop, or even very popular, but Mrs Leigh Perrot liked to go there because the prices were comparatively reasonable. The assistants seemed civil and obliging, and when Mrs Leigh Perrot called to buy some black lace, they were delighted to serve her and found exactly what was required. Mrs Leigh Perrot was able to congratulate herself on making a very satisfactory purchase comparatively cheaply, until soon afterwards, as she and her husband were walking slowly along the street together, one of the shop assistants appeared at her elbow and made the incredible accusation that the parcel she was carrying under her arm contained some lace which she had stolen. Naturally Mrs Leigh Perrot was indignant. She denied the charge absolutely, but when the parcel was opened, it proved to contain a card of white lace in addition to the black lace which she had purchased.

It was a common enough trick. Mr and Mrs Leigh Perrot were known to be wealthy, respectable people, who valued their reputation very highly. Surely they would never risk a court case, with all the publicity involved, let alone the possibility of spending some time in prison before the trial. They would be only too glad to silence the shopkeeper by handing over a substantial sum of money. It was pure blackmail, but the people at the shop thought it was a safe bet. So it might have been with some wealthy folk, but not with Mr and Mrs Leigh Perrot.

Two days later, a complaint was laid before the magistrates, who had no option but to commit Mrs Leigh Perrot for trial. The next assizes would be held at Taunton in the following March, eight months away, and meanwhile she must lie in Ilchester Jail. It was an appalling situation. The penalty for theft was hanging, or if a reprieve was granted, transportation to Botany Bay for fourteen years. Mrs Leigh Perrot refused to be daunted; she steadfastly maintained her innocence and her devoted husband stood by her. If she must go to prison, he would go too; if she were to be transported, he would sell his property and accompany her over the seas. The fortitude of the couple and their utter loyalty to one another were beyond praise.

Mr Leigh Perrot managed to mitigate the worst conditions of his wife's imprisonment. He paid for them both to lodge with the chief jailor and his wife, Mr and Mrs Scadding, and there they remained until the trial. Mr and Mrs Scadding made them as comfortable as they could, but their quarters were small and their family was large; the children seemed to be everywhere and the Leigh Perrots were not used to children, even at the best of times. Poor Mrs Scadding realized that Mrs Leigh Perrot, like all rich folk, was inclined to be fussy about her food, so she did her best to oblige her. Wealthy people disliked using the same table implements for different things, she thought, so she was careful to lick the knife clean from the fried onions before she plunged it into the butter. Even this did not seem to please the lady, but at least Mrs Scadding had done her best.

Mrs Austen made herself ill with worrying about her sister; she even offered to send Cassandra and Jane to look after their aunt and uncle. James was terribly concerned and wished to attend the trial, but he broke his leg in a riding accident and was immobilized at home. Mrs Leigh Perrot refused to allow her nieces – "those elegant young women" as she called them – to be shut up with her in Mr and Mrs Scadding's sordid little home, and as for allowing them to sit with her in court, she would not hear of such a thing. "To have two young creatures gazed at in a public court would cut me to the very heart," she said.

It took the jury at Taunton less than a quarter of an hour to find Mrs Leigh Perrot not guilty. That was the end of the whole hideous affair, except for the general rejoicing which followed her release. Even that may not have been quite the end, however. Jane, who so enjoyed shopping for pretty trifles, who wrote with such delight to Cassandra about her purchases, who would draw the pattern of a lace border for a cloak in one of her letters, never seemed to be able to conquer her unaccountable dislike of Bath.

7

THE AUSTENS WERE full of plans for improvements at the parsonage. Possibly there was a little money to spare, now that all the Austen sons were well established. Frank and Charles were both doing well in the navy; Frank had even been promoted again, though news travelled so slowly that his family knew all about it long before he did. Jane wrote to Cassandra at Godmersham about the new trees to be planted in the garden and the scheme for a new orchard with apples, pears and cherries. Did Cassandra approve of this idea, wrote Jane? Or would ornamental trees be better? The furniture in the house was being re-arranged to accommodate supplementary purchases; some new tables were a great success; they could be put together to form one large table or the two ends could be joined to make a neat oval table which could be used for all ordinary purposes. Jane sent a full description of everything to Cassandra, who was staying even longer than usual with Edward and Elizabeth. Cassandra was absolutely indispensable at Godmersham every time a new baby was born into the family circle, but Jane was longing for her to return home so that they could discuss all these new arrangements and enjoy moving the furniture round together.

One day during Cassandra's absence, they had an alarming experience. A wild storm swept across the countryside, leaving a trail of damage and bringing the two great elms near the parsonage crashing down. Jane could not help teasing Cassandra with the information that solemn James Digweed had assured her that the elms had fallen "from their grief at your absence," adding "was it not a galant idea?" It was quite safe to tease Cassandra about James Digweed. Everybody knew that Cassandra's heart was buried in San Domingo.

Jane was missing Cassandra even more than usual. She felt restless, and as her parents seemed to be in good health at present, there could surely be no harm in planning a little visit to Martha at Ibthorpe. She might even persuade Martha to return with her to Steventon. Failing Cassandra, Martha was a good companion for a chatter. Martha wondered if Jane might find it dull at Ibthorpe, so she suggested she might bring a few books with her, but Jane rejected the idea in her next letter with a cascade of delicious nonsense.

> I come to you to be talked to, not to read or hear reading – I can do *that* at home; and indeed I am now laying in a stock of intelligence to pour out on you as *my* share of Conversation. – I am reading Henry's *History of England*, which I will repeat to you in any manner you may prefer, either in a loose, desultary, unconnected strain, or dividing my recital as the Historian divides it himself, into seven parts, The Civil & Military – Religion – Constitution – Learning & Learned Men – Arts & Sciences – Commerce Coins & Shipping & Manners; – so that for every evening of the week there will be a different subject; the friday's lot, Commerce, Coin & Shipping, You will find the least entertaining; but the next Eveng:'s portion will make amends. – With such a provision on my part, if you will do yours by repeating the French Grammar, & Mrs. Stent will now & then ejaculate some

wonder about the Cocks & Hens, – what can we want for?

Mrs Stent was a widow in poor circumstances who lived with Mrs Lloyd; she was a great talker in a disjointed way, and the girls derived a good deal of quiet amusement from her random incursions into the conversation.

The visit passed happily if uneventfully, and Martha fell in with the plan that she should return to Steventon with Jane. They actually planned to travel by themselves in a post chaise; the distance was only twenty miles but even so, it was something of an event to embark on such a journey without an escort. They arrived at the parsonage in high spirits; Jane could not wait to show Martha the new arrangements. It would be almost as good as discussing them with Cassandra.

Mrs Austen welcomed them joyfully. "Well, girls," she said. "It is all settled. We have decided to leave Steventon and go to live at Bath."

That was all. There was nothing to make a fuss about. It seemed to Mrs Austen the most natural thing in the world. Jane did not find it so. With a sudden exclamation, a catching of the breath, she slid to the floor. For the first time in her life, she had fainted.

It was a long time before she recovered from the shock. Nobody was ever to know how she felt about it, because long afterwards, when Cassandra was an old lady, she destroyed all the letters Jane wrote to her during those first few weeks after the decision had been made. It was the end of a chapter. She was twenty-five years old and all her life so far had been spent in Steventon. All her friends were there, or at least not far away; all her happy memories of childhood were centred at the parsonage, and the unhappy ones had faded in the sanctuary of that well-loved home; the world outside might wound you, but the wound would never be mortal so long as that sure refuge remained. She

83

could not imagine life without it. There was the other life too, the imaginary world which belonged to that little sitting room upstairs, with the shabby furniture and the worn carpet. Was she to lose that also?

After a few weeks of inward turmoil, Jane managed to face the inevitable, and having faced it, she could make light of it. After all, she suggested to Cassandra, they had lived long enough in Steventon; the Basingstoke balls were "on the decline", and there was a good deal of excitement and entertainment to be gained from planning the move and deciding where their new home was to be. They did not want to live too near the Leigh Perrots, but it was important to choose a house in a good part of the town, preferably with open spaces at hand, so that they would not feel shut in. They could not afford to live in one of the more fashionable neighbourhoods, or even near Paragon, but their choice was not limited too much by their means; Mr Austen looked to enjoying an income of about six hundred pounds a year when he retired and this should be ample for them to live in comfort, if not in affluence. Jane wrote to Cassandra that they should be able to keep two maids and a manservant. "We plan having a steady Cook", she wrote, "and a young giddy Housemaid, with a sedate, middle-aged Man who is to undertake the double office of Husband to the former and sweetheart to the latter. – No children of course to be allowed on either side."

Certainly Jane was irrepressible. She flared up, however, when even her nearest and dearest made suggestions about the disposal of her treasured possessions. James was to succeed his father in the living, and he and Mary were full of plans for their removal from Deane to Steventon. Mrs Austen and Cassandra both thought it would be a good idea for Jane to leave her treasured cabinet behind for little Anna, who was just the right age to enjoy having such a piece of furniture for her very own. "You are very kind in planning presents for me to make," wrote Jane to Cassandra, "and my mother has shown me exactly the same attention – but as I do not chuse to have Generosity dictated to me, I shall not resolve on giving my cabinet to Anna till the first thought of it has been my own."

Nearly all the furniture was to be sold, including Jane's piano, but not their beds – they all valued their comfort too highly to risk buying new beds. Otherwise transport was so costly that they would have to part with even their most treasured pieces. It would be cheaper to buy what they wanted in Bath. Even the books must go, and Jane tried hard to persuade James to buy his father's library at half a guinea a volume. James was far too cautious to fall in with this idea. He waited for the valuation and bought the entire library for seventy pounds. It was hard to part with the books, especially for Jane, who had to part with those she had collected since childhood, but doubtless the Austens would find all the reading matter they required in the excellent lending libraries which abounded in Bath. In the eyes of the older generation, Bath as a place of residence left nothing to be desired. Mrs Austen could hardly wait to get there.

As yet they had nowhere to live. Uncle and Aunt Leigh Perrot invited Mrs Austen and Jane to stay with them until they found a house to their liking; Mr Austen was planning a round of visits and Cassandra was still at Godmersham. The Leigh Perrots were obviously still hoping that the Austens would settle somewhere near them, and in all their proffered help in house-hunting they had this in mind. Jane was still determined to find a suitable house in some other part of the town, but she enjoyed staying at Number 1 Paragon more than she usually did. She had a comfortable room to herself up two flights of stairs, and her uncle and aunt were uniformly kind, especially her uncle, who was eager for news of Frank and Charles and seemed to treasure every scrap of information she could produce. Jane always loved to talk about her sailor brothers.

In the intervals between examining what she described as "putrifying houses", Jane joined in some of the social activities of the town and made a few friends. One of these was a lady whom she and Cassandra had known slightly on some previous occasion. Before leaving home, Jane had written to tell Cassandra that Mr and Mrs Chamberlayn were in Bath. They were "lodging at the Charitable Repository", she wrote, adding: "I wish the scene may suggest to Mrs. C the notion of selling her black beaver bonnet for the releif of the poor." Obviously Mrs Chamberlayn did not share Jane's interest in becoming headgear, but she was more than her equal in her love for cross-country walks. Jane sent Cassandra a breathless account of a walk to Weston, a village less than two miles to the north-west of Bath.

> It would have amused you to see our progress; – we went up by Sion Hill, and turned across the field; – in climbing a hill Mrs. Chamberlayn is very capital; I could with difficulty keep pace with her – yet would not flinch for the world. – On plain ground I was quite her equal – and so we posted away under the fine hot sun, *She* without any parasol or any shade to her hat, stopping for nothing, and Crossing the Church Yard at Weston with as much expedition as if we were afraid of being buried alive. – after seeing what she is equal to, I cannot help feeling a regard for her.

On a later occasion they took a walk in the opposite direction, to Lyncombe Hill and Widcombe Old Church, when "Mrs. Chamberlayn's pace was not quite so magnificent". But not long afterwards the energetic lady and her husband left Bath and the brief friendship was over.

Jane seemed restless and dissatisfied, picking up a friendship here and there, and discarding it with little effort or regret. There appeared to be very little sparkle about the balls and dances, and the smaller parties were insufferably dull. Even the local gossip and scandal provided very little excitement, though to be sure Jane did not miss much of it. She found that she had "a very good eye at an Adulteress, for though repeatedly assured that another in the same party was the *She*, I fixed upon the right one from the first". In the Upper Rooms she watched with mild interest a tipsy wife pursuing her drunken husband; this kind of behaviour afforded some amusement to the spectator, but it was too common to be anything but boring. She met a couple called Mr and Mrs Evelyn who were friendly and helpful; Mr Evelyn's name had been connected with the "She" of doubtful reputation, but he seemed harmless enough, and when he invited her for a drive in his "very bewitching Phaeton and four", Jane could not resist such an attractive invitation. She thoroughly enjoyed the drive to the top of Kingsdown and back, and her pleasure was enhanced by the surprise which awaited her on her return – a letter from Charles, who had received thirty pounds as his share of the prize money for taking a privateer, and expected ten pounds more. "But of what avail is it to take prizes if he lays out the produce in presents for his sisters?" demanded Jane. "He has been buying gold chains and Topaze crosses for us; – he must be well scolded." The sisters treasured those gold chains and topaz crosses for the rest of their lives.

The house eventually chosen by the Austens, Number 4 Sydney Place, was in a new part of the town, across the river and overlooking the then fashionable Sydney Gardens. It was reached by Pulteney Bridge, and the houses were new and well built, unlike those "putrifying houses" with their "damp offices", which Jane had grown so tired of inspecting. They would not be able to move into their new home until after their summer holiday, which they spent at Sidmouth. One of the attractions of their removal, and Mr

Austen's retirement, had been that they would be able to spend their holidays by the sea. They repeated the experiment next year, staying at Dawlish and Teignmouth, and to this day nobody knows for certain which of these places had a special significance for Jane, though all the evidence, such as it is, points to Sidmouth. All traces of the occurrence have been removed from her letters, and in any case none has survived for the relevant and the immediately succeeding years. Cassandra kept the secret inviolate until, long after Jane's death, a chance encounter brought about a momentary break in her apparently impenetrable reserve.

Caroline Austen, Anna's half-sister, never forgot the incident. She and her mother, and Aunt Cassandra, were all staying at Newtown in Montgomeryshire when they met a singularly attractive and handsome young man. Aunt Cassandra seemed to take a quite extraordinary liking for him. This in itself was unusual. Cassandra seldom took an interest in strangers. Soon after leaving Newtown, they heard that the young man had died very suddenly, and the news shook Aunt Cassandra out of her usual composure. She was so upset that they were alarmed and begged to know the reason for her great distress, until at last she could maintain her silence no longer. "He was so like . . . and to die so suddenly . . . just like . . ." At last the story came out. Long ago, when they had been staying at the seaside in Devonshire with their parents, she and her sister had met just such an attractive and handsome man, the brother of the local doctor, whom they already knew. The resemblance to this other young man had been so striking as to bring the whole incident vividly to her mind. He and Jane had fallen deeply in love. This was not Tom Lefroy's "boyish love", or the first romantic love of a young girl; it was the mature love which needs no words to express it, the love which can spring from a second attachment when the first has passed softly into memory, the love which can flower quickly into a perfect understanding.

Cassandra watched this happening and accepted the inevitability of the outcome. The close bond between the sisters would be broken and Jane would enter into a new life in which she would have no share. She was still struggling with her mixed emotions when they left the Devonshire resort and the lovers were parted; she had not mastered them when the news came that the young man was dead.

Nobody will ever know what Jane owed to Cassandra during the tragic weeks which followed. Nobody will ever know the whole truth of the story. Only through Jane's exquisite understanding of true constancy can the significance of it be grasped.

There was one curious aftermath. Possibly on account of a visible depression of spirit, Cassandra and Jane left Bath for some weeks to visit James and Mary. Doubtless the Leigh Perrots could be depended on to provide companionship for Mr and Mrs Austen. All their friends in the neighbourhood of Steventon were delighted to see the sisters and they were showered with invitations. One of these was an invitation to stay for a while at Manydown House, the hospitable home where they used to spend the night, when they went to balls at Basingstoke with their friends Elizabeth, Catherine and Alethea Bigg. What fun they had enjoyed after the dancing, chattering about their partners, and the ridiculous fashions worn by some of the older people, let alone the latest gossip, featherlight and innocuous! That had been long ago, and now they were all grown up; Elizabeth had been married five years previously but was now a widow; Catherine and Alethea were still at home and overjoyed to see their old friends again. Harrison Bigg-Wither, the schoolboy brother of the old days, was now nearly twenty-two, a rather delicate but decidedly pleasant young man, much sought after as the heir of Manydown. Gone were the days when he had been poor little Harrison, shoved aside and left out of the conversation because he could not possibly understand what the girls were chattering about, or share their secrets.

One evening Jane had an unexpected shock. Snatching an opportunity when the others were absent, Harrison suddenly overcame his reserve completely. He told her that he had loved her all his life and that he would always love her; that the discrepancy in their ages meant absolutely nothing to him; that she was the only woman he could ever marry and that he adored her.

Jane listened in amazement. She could not but be impressed by the young man's adoration. She was stirred by compassion for his struggle with the emotions which seemed to be tearing him to pieces. Her own struggle was over. At the back of her mind was an awareness that she had known young love and mature love and lost them both; there could be nothing left for her but warm affection, and this she felt. Of course she loved young Harrison – as his sisters loved him. And here he was, begging her to be his wife and the mistress of Manydown House. Why should she ask more of life than that? She would have a kind, loving husband, a beautiful and familiar house, sisters-in-law who loved her, and a home for Cassandra when her parents were no more. All this was within her grasp. She had only to reach out her hand to Harrison and take it. Why should she leave Harrison in agonizing suspense? Why should she hesitate?

Suddenly Jane capitulated. She put the past behind her and said yes. Any sensible woman would have said the same. Not many girls in those days could marry for love; they were far more likely to marry for an establishment, just as the young men were likely to marry for money. "Never marry for money," as the old north-country saying goes, "but let thi heart rest where money bides."

In the night came misgivings, and then a turmoil of spirits which made sleep out of the question. What had she done? She argued with herself through the small hours. Yes, this was probably her last chance of marriage. Yes, she was no longer young, and this proposal was surely the last she would ever receive. Yes, he loved her and had always loved her. Was it not possible that she would come to love him in return? And if not, surely many comfortable marriages could jog along happily enough, untouched by romance? She was not asking for perfection, only for a little happiness, and surely marriage with Harrison would give her that? Back and forth the arguments went until at last she roused Cassandra. She could bear it no longer. She had decided to take back her word.

James and Mary were about their usual tasks at the parsonage next morning when suddenly the Manydown carriage drove up and stopped at the door. Whatever could this mean? Had one of the sisters been taken ill? The pair alighted hurriedly, but the carriage did not wait. It rumbled away in the direction of Basingstoke as Cassandra and Jane entered the house in tears.

The event must have been a sad blow for James and Mary. To have Jane happily married and comfortably settled in their own neighbourhood must have seemed to them a perfect prospect, and one for which they may even have been secretly hoping. The situation must have been beyond their comprehension. And now Jane, shaken with sobs, was begging to be conveyed home to her parents at once. No, she could not remain in Steventon, no, she must go right away at once – at once – please, please would James order the carriage and take her home? Nothing could have been more inconvenient for a country clergyman who was expected to preach on Sunday and must find a substitute if unable to do so. But James and Mary were understanding – far more so than later critics have given them credit for. Their compassion for Jane outweighed any irritation they may have felt at this unexpected outcome of the eagerly anticipated visit. James ordered the horses to be put up and took his sisters back to Bath.

There have been hints of other possible romances – a deduction from a stray sentence in a letter, a rumour of family activity in building castles in the air. All these left Jane heart-whole. She was never to betray herself again, never to lose the balance which comes from perfect self-control. Always there would be sympathy amongst their intimate friends for Cassandra's sad story, but nobody would be allowed to guess at Jane's. She would carry her secret with her to the grave. Like the chief captain who questioned St Paul, she had paid a great price for her freedom.

8

THERE ARE PERIODS in life which might perhaps be described as "waiting" periods. Nothing very much happens, or if something does occur, the significance of it is not immediately apparent. Somebody has dropped the jigsaw puzzle, and it cannot be put together successfully until the pattern has been found.

During these years at Bath, even public events of considerable importance seemed difficult to evaluate. In 1802, the Austens, like everybody else, rejoiced at the signing of the Peace of Amiens. It was true that it did not seem to be a very favourable treaty so far as the hard-pressed British were concerned, but at least the war was over, and that ambitious general, Napoleon Buonaparte, First Consul of France, had been appeased. "Boney" was a name to conjure with. People in the south of England had lived too long in dread of an invasion and now at last they could relax. The Austens were probably as pleased as everybody else, except that the direct result of the Peace, so far as they were concerned, was that Frank was put on half-pay, and that Henry resigned from the militia so that his military career was at an end.

Eliza was overjoyed when the treaty was signed. At last she would be able to cross the Channel and try to claim her husband's estates. Henry may not have been so sure, but he was a kind, understanding husband, and he may have felt that his wife would benefit from a complete change of scene involving a definite plan of action, after the death of poor little Hastings. Nobody seems to have guessed that the Peace of Amiens would be short lived. War broke out again in the following May, and Henry and Eliza were very nearly trapped and interned, with all the other English travellers who had been unable to resist the temptation to re-visit France. Only Eliza's perfect French saved them. Henry lolled back in the carriage, pretending to be a surly, boorish husband, and the charming Eliza won the hearts of all the officials who tried to hold them up on the suspicion that they might be English. *Anglais? Impossible! Mille pardons Madame*! they would say, and the carriage would roll on towards the coast with handsome Henry suddenly transformed once more into the most loving and attentive husband that she could have desired. They never regained Eliza's estates, and they arrived home with little more than they stood up in, but at least they were safely back in England.

Frank was glad to be in action again. At first he was sent to organize the Sea Fencibles, from the headquarters which had been set up for them at Ramsgate. The Sea Fencibles were a special force intended to guard the coast against invasion. They were a motley crowd and Frank must sometimes have thought, "God help England if Boney invades!" but at least he did his best to lick them into shape before he went to sea again. Meanwhile there were attractions to be found in Ramsgate, especially when he was invited to visit the home of a family called Gibson. By the time he left Ramsgate, he and Mary Gibson were engaged, but there could be no thought of marriage while the future was so uncertain. Meanwhile Jane visited Ramsgate before Frank went off to sea again, and was delighted with her future sister-in-law. This says a great deal for Mary Gibson, because Frank's sisters had always hoped that he would marry Martha Lloyd.

During the earlier months of their stay in Bath, Mrs Austen was seriously ill and required constant nursing. Cassandra and Jane, under the direction of the local medical man, Mr Bowen, managed to pull her through, and once the worst was over the old lady was as lively as ever and even wrote comic verses to celebrate her recovery.

Says Death: "I've been trying these three weeks and more
To seize on old madam here at number four,
Yet I still try in vain, though she's turned of three score,
*   To what is my ill success owing?"*
"I'll tell you, old Fellow, if you cannot guess,
To what you're indebted for your ill success –
To the prayers of my husband, whose love I possess,
To the care of my daughters, whom Heaven will bless,
*   To the skill and attention of Bowen."*

At such a time all Jane's energies were called into action; otherwise life at Bath limped along in a rather monotonous way, and the girls must often have remembered the full and happy life at the parsonage, with all the comings and goings of young people, and all the affairs of the parish to claim their attention. Most of all, they must have missed the fun and laughter in the little upstairs sitting room. The manuscripts were still there in Jane's writing desk, and sometimes she would read through them. One day she suddenly decided to do something about them. First impressions, her favourite, had already been rejected; she could not bear to have it rejected again. *Sense and Sensibility* needed more revision. But what about *Susan*? Surely *Susan* might appeal to some publisher; it would be sure to attract plenty of readers in Bath.

This time she did not enlist her father's help. He was in failing health, and also she was never quite sure if he had gone the right way about it when he approached Cadell. Instead, she gave *Susan* a quick revision and entrusted the manuscript to Henry. Henry was supposed to have a good head for business, which was more than his father had, and he had always appreciated Jane's literary efforts. Apparently, she could not have done better or taken a wiser step. *Susan* was accepted at once by a publisher called Crosby, who bought the manuscript outright for ten pounds. This seemed like untold wealth to Jane. Her annual allowance was twenty pounds and here she was with half as much again. Moreover, Crosby advertised its publication as imminent, and Jane could hardly wait to see her creation transformed into two neat volumes on the library shelves. The wait was tantalizing; soon it became frustrating; and eventually it seemed that Mr Crosby had changed his mind, for nothing happened and the book did not appear. Six years later, Jane tried to get the manuscript back, but without success. All she could do was to revise her own fair copy and hope for better times.

One thing stood out in this rather monotonous period and that was the holiday Jane spent with her parents at Lyme Regis. Certain holidays leave a special imprint on the memory – the place, the scenery, the people, and that indefinable sensation of "never again". It was just the perfect, halcyon period which sometimes comes before the breaking of a link.

After their return the Austens moved house again. Mr Austen was now too frail to attempt the daily walk from Sydney Place to the Pump Room, so they took up new quarters in Green Park Buildings. The neighbourhood was not particularly fashionable, but the houses were comfortable enough and they had a pleasant view over the Green Park, down by the river Avon. Perhaps they were rather too near the river for comfort, especially in winter, when the mist rose and the flooded banks were sodden, but again this seemed to be a waiting period in their lives; they were never to associate happiness with that house in Green Park Buildings. There Jane celebrated her twenty-ninth birthday, which was to be the last birthday of which she would have only happy recollections, for on that day, as they learnt later, her dear friend, Mrs Lefroy, was thrown from her horse and killed instantaneously. This was a terrible shock for the Austens, and most of all for Jane. Madame Lefroy had influenced her since childhood; she had loved her and encouraged her; moreover she had understood her at a time when other people had been critical, seeing only the shy, awkward, impulsive, wayward little girl, so much less attractive than Cassandra. With Mrs Lefroy she had always held first place, and the strong friendship which had grown up between them had been a formative influence in her life. The brutal manner of her death seemed to strike abruptly against every happy memory. It would be a long time before Jane recovered from this sudden loss.

There was little comfort to be found elsewhere. The news from the outside world was seldom encouraging, with the growing menace of Napoleon's power threatening Europe. He had recently been declared Emperor of the French, and France acclaimed this aggrandizement unequivocally as the first step in a glorious era of world power, which would involve the utter downfall of Britain. There were continuing threats of invasion, with only the British navy standing between the British people and disaster. And Frank and Charles were both in the navy, apparently as light-hearted as the young pilots in the Battle of Britain in a later era, and every bit as confident of victory. Their sisters, however, were soon preoccupied with a more immediate problem, nearer home. Mr Austen's health did not improve, though he seldom or never complained. He seemed quite happy in his daily routine and had complete faith in the excellent Mr Bowen, who had done so much for his wife. The family had no special cause for anxiety. Even when one of his customary attacks came on, with fever and headache and violent trembling, they were not instantly alarmed. Mr Bowen gave the usual treatment, and for a while he seemed to recover, but next day his condition worsened, and Mr Bowen sent for a skilled physician, Dr Gibbs. All was done that could be done, but to no avail. After a long period of unconsciousness, George Austen, the poor relation who had made good, the Handsome Proctor, the dearly loved rector and teacher, died peacefully with a smile on his lips. "His tenderness as a father, who can do justice to?" wrote Jane, when she broke the news to Frank, away at sea. That tenderness she would miss for the rest of her life.

There were immediate problems to be faced. The Austens had never been rich; now they were likely to be poor. Mr Austen's stipend died with him, and his wife and daughters were faced with the possibility of having to live on an income of two hundred and ten pounds a year. Letters sped between the sons as each tried to see what could be done to augment that meagre income. Edward was in a position to offer a hundred pounds a year, which was gratefully accepted. There would be no difficulty for him in guaranteeing such a sum. Francis at first offered the same, but obviously he could not possibly afford it and the sum was reduced to fifty pounds. James and Henry both offered fifty pounds, which brought the annual income to four hundred and sixty pounds. Optimistic Henry thought that such a sum would solve all Mrs Austen's financial problems, but very sensibly she decided to leave her present quarters and take modest lodgings in Gay Street, which would be cheaper, and where only one maid would be required. Gay Street was a very pleasant part of the town, but Bath itself had few attractions for them now. They were to make one more move, to Trim Street, before leaving the city for good in 1805.

It was while they were at Gay Street that Martha Lloyd agreed to come and live with them. Her mother had died after a long illness, and her friendship with the Austen girls encouraged her to think that she could live with them more happily than with Eliza or Mary. Apart from their pleasure in her companionship, Cassandra and Jane looked to derive a good deal of benefit from this arrangement. It would have been impossible for them both to be away from home at any time in the future, had not this kindly "third sister" made herself available to look after Mrs Austen.

Two years after leaving Bath, Jane mentioned in a letter to Cassandra their "happy feelings of escape". A place from which you long to escape is not an ideal setting for creative writing. Add to this the heights of joy, the depths of sorrow, and the grim monotony experienced in that place, and surely you need not look further for the reason why Jane wrote so little during those years in Bath. In a sudden burst of energy she had asked Henry to dispose of *Susan* on her behalf; he had done so successfully and nothing had come of it. There was no encouragement to be gained there. In another burst of energy she had made a fair copy of *Lady Susan*, but this did not satisfy her. She would have framed it differently had she been writing it afresh. Then she suddenly spurred herself into action; she began a new story which was in full flight when interrupted, first by Mrs Lefroy's death, and then by her father's last illness. After that she had not the heart to pick it up again. Besides which, it went a little too near the bone.

The story was called *The Watsons*, and the heroine was a lovely, portionless girl called Emma Watson. One of the most delightful scenes in any of Jane Austen's stories come in an early chapter of the book, giving the lie to all those later critics who said she did not like children. A ten-year-old boy, who is "uncommonly fond of dancing", is brought to a ball by his widowed mother, with a company of local aristocrats from the Castle. Emma notices his extreme excitement and then overhears his mother explaining the reason to one of her friends. The beautiful Miss Osborne, sister of Lord Osborne, has promised him the first two dances. "Oh yes," cries the boy. "We have been engaged this week and we are to dance down every couple!" He can hardly wait for the music to begin, and Emma watches with delight the animated expression on his face. Then everything suddenly changes. Miss Osborne pauses at his side for a moment and explains that she must break the engagement; she will be dancing those first dances – the most important ones – with Colonel Beresford, but never mind, she will dance with him later on, after tea. For the child the light goes out. "If the poor little boy's face had in its happiness been interesting to Emma, it was infinitely more so under the sudden reverse; he stood the picture of disappointment, with crimson cheeks, quivering lips, and eyes bent on the floor." He tries to pretend that he does not mind, but try as he will, he cannot hide his disappointment. Then Emma steps forward. "I shall be very happy to dance with you, sir, if you like it," she says and so sweeps the child from the depths of humiliation and distress to the heights of joy. "Oh uncle," he cries later on as they thread their way through the fashionable crowd. "Do look at my partner. She is so pretty!"

All this has its influence on the plot, which was never to be completed, but the little scene itself immortalized the feelings of a child whose trust has been betrayed. It also shows that in her portrayal of children, Jane Austen was far ahead of her time. This realization of a child as a person; this sensitive grasp of a child's reaction both to disappointment and to joy; this complete identification with a child's mind which momentarily sees in turn the disappointment and the joy as going on for ever; one would have to look a long way to find these in the novels of Jane Austen's contemporaries, or of her immediate successors.

Although Jane never finished the story, she had worked out the plot and, as usual, she shared it with Cassandra. It was an admirable plot and would probably have been made even better. It is true that Emma's father was to die early in the book, and as Jane's father died while she was writing it, her grief may be supposed to have brought the story to a sudden stop. It is true that Emma's unhappiness in her surroundings may echo too closely Cassandra and Jane's unhappiness in Bath. There may, however, be another explanation. When you raise a heavy stone, you are sometimes first fascinated, and then repelled, by the crawling life revealed underneath it. There is something of the same sensation to be found in Jane's exploration of the feelings of the unmarried sisters, Elizabeth, Margaret and Penelope Watson. Their father is ailing and cannot provide for them; outwardly pleasant, sensible young women, there is nothing they will not do to catch a husband. They buoy themselves up with false hopes; they set off in frantic pursuit of any eligible male; they will scratch one another's eyes out if prevented from making a conquest. Elizabeth, the eldest, left behind in the chase, has long put aside all thoughts of romance. "I think I could like any good-humoured man with a comfortable income," she says resignedly.

The stone must be put down quickly to hide what lies beneath. At first it seemed fascinating; now it is repellent. Jane was not yet ready to present her immortal picture of spinsterhood. Only in her reply to a letter from Cassandra, who was staying with Martha Lloyd after Mrs Lloyd's death, she commented on some reference to that tiresome, loquacious friend of Mrs Lloyd's, Mrs Stent, an elderly widow of long standing. "Poor Mrs. Stent! It has been her lot to be always in the way; but we must be merciful, for perhaps in time we may come to be Mrs. Stents ourselves, unequal to anything and unwelcome to everybody." It was a harsh judgement, but at least it contained a hint of compassion. Not until that compassion had grown into compassionate understanding would Jane be able to portray the fate of an ageing woman left alone in the world.

9

I T HAS SOMETIMES been fashionable to criticize Cassandra and
Jane for apparently showing so little interest in the great events
of their time. Perhaps if Jane had known that every line of her
surviving letters would be scrutinized by exacting critics, she
would have written to Cassandra at length about the threat of
invasion, and Napoleon's latest victories, and the state of the economy, instead of chatting away about their nephews and nieces, or
the prices paid for muslin and lace and the making up of gowns, or
the curious behaviour of some of their neighbours. It is more
likely, however, that if she had had the slightest suspicion of what
was to come, Jane would have told Cassandra to burn all her letters
and leave the curiosity of posterity unsatisfied. In any case, people
living in the turmoil of great events do not necessarily write about
them to their nearest and dearest, unless they are personally
involved. The sisters were quick enough to share every detail of
information about the movements of their brothers' ships, or to
speculate as to how they would be affected by the events of the
day. At the time of Corunna, Jane wondered in one of her letters
whether Frank would be involved in the evacuation of "what may
remain by this time of our poor army whose state seems dreadfully
critical". In another she exclaimed "Thank Heaven we have had
no one to care for particularly among the troops," and a little later

on: "How horrible to have so many people killed! – and what a blessing that one cares for none of them!" Some twentieth-century readers throw up their hands in horror at such heartless sentiments, as if they had never heaved sighs of relief on finding that none of their loved ones had been involved in some particular accident or disaster.

Before this, Frank had one sad disappointment. Owing to contrary winds, his ship did not arrive on the scene at Trafalgar in time to take part in the battle. He had foreseen that this might happen. He had written to his dearest Mary explaining that he was not inclined to vainglory, or fighting for fighting's sake, but it did seem hard that when he and his companions had borne the heat and burden of the day for so long, they should miss this stupendous victory. The death of Nelson was a stunning blow. Frank's admiration of the little Admiral was intense, and he never again expected to see such a man and such a leader.

Frank's chosen career suited him well, and he and his brother Charles were both to distinguish themselves in the service of the Royal Navy. As young men, both seem to have been affectionate and home-loving; it was typical of Frank that when he came ashore in 1806 and married his Mary, he should decide that the best thing for everybody concerned would be for him to find a nice roomy house in Southampton, so that his wife, his mother, his sisters and their friend Martha Lloyd could all live there together while he was away at sea. Not may newly-wed husbands would have thought this to be a good idea.

By the time Frank found his nice large house in Southampton, his mother and sisters had long left Bath with relief, but they filled in the time pleasantly enough with brief stays in lodgings and with family visits. One memorable visit was to Stoneleigh Abbey, which belonged to a branch of Mrs Austen's family. The owner, Lord Leigh, had died and the succession was in dispute; there was no direct heir and the will indicated that the Reverend Thomas Leigh, rector of Adlestrop, was to succeed, though the direction was not quite clear. Other members of the family were believed to have some claim on this large estate, including Mr Leigh Perrot, who gave up his for a payment of £24,000 down and an additional £2,000 a year. Quite how Mrs Austen and her daughters, who were having a constant struggle to live within their small income, felt about this vast enrichment of relations who were already very wealthy, is not known, though much may be imagined. However, they all enjoyed staying at Stoneleigh Abbey with the Reverend Thomas Leigh; he had been advised to take possession of the disputed inheritance immediately, and as the Austens were staying with him at the time, they naturally joined the party. Stoneleigh Abbey was a huge place, far bigger than Godmersham; Mrs Austen humorously suggested that the heir had better put up a signpost in the vast corridors, as his guests were perpetually losing their way.

When at last they were ready to move into the big house at Southampton, Cassandra was at Godmersham and the rest of the family became impatient for her return. How could they cope with everything that was involved without her help and advice? "Frank and Mary cannot at all approve of your not being at home in time to help them with their furnishing purchases," wrote Jane. Indeed they threatened to be "as spiteful as possible and chuse everything in the stile most likely to vex you, knives that will not cut, glasses that will not hold, a sofa without a seat and a Bookcase without shelves". Cassandra was not even there in time to help with planning the garden. True, they had found a gardener, "a Man who bears a remarkably good character, has a good complexion and asks something less than the first". He was very emphatic about the poor quality of the roses and the suitable position for the planting of soft fruit, but he had to be persuaded by Jane to procure some syringas – "I could not do without a syringa for the sake of Cowper's line." She was thinking of one of Cowper's poems in which he speaks of "syringa, ivory pure".

In spite of Cassandra's absence, they managed to settle in very happily and everything was soon ship-shape, as any project planned by Frank was bound to be. He seemed to be able to turn his hand to anything. Even when he was kept indoors by a cough he set to work to make "a very nice fringe for the drawing room curtains". Jane's other sailor brother, Charles, was married at about this time to Frances Palmer, daughter of the Governor-General of Bermuda, but there could be no question yet of setting up house; for reasons of convenience and of economy the young couple decided to live afloat, and it seems possible that Mrs Croft in *Persuasion* may have been drawing on their experience when she declared that she knew "nothing superior to the accommodation of a man-of-war – the happiest part of my life has been spent on board a ship".

Jane's letters at this time are full of descriptions of comings and goings, and people calling or not calling, of visits paid and returned, and even of elopements in high life. And then there were the children – like the little girl brought home by Frank one morning after church: "she is now talking away by my side and examining the Treasures of my Writing-desk drawer – very happy, I beleive – not at all shy, of course." Remembering the agonies of shyness she had experienced in her own childish days, Jane wondered "what is become of all the Shyness in the world?" She was not critical, only curious. She spent most of the afternoon playing spillikins with the little girl. Jane was neat-fingered, and the careful balancing and withdrawal of the delicate ivory spillikins was brought by her to a fine art. The child blossomed in her company and Jane, watching her quietly, drew her own conclusions. "She is a nice, natural, open-hearted affectionate girl, with all the ready civility which one sees in the best Children in the present day; – so unlike anything that I was myself at her age that I am often all astonishment and shame."

A little boy who stayed there left a vivid description of the house as he remembered it, long afterwards. This was Edward Austen, James's son, then not quite ten years old; he and his little sister Caroline, had been staying at Godmersham with their parents and their Aunt Jane. There was a flock of cousins of all ages at Godmersham now, from fifteen-year-old Fanny down to two-year-old Cassandra Jane; the little brother and sister from Steventon had never had so many playmates in their lives. Edward had enjoyed himself, but his observant Aunt Jane had noticed that three-year-old Caroline was somewhat overwhelmed. "I believe the little girl will be glad to go home; – her cousins are too much for her." Young Edward, on the other hand, was delighted at the prospect of visiting his grandmother in Southampton before returning home, especially as this involved travelling with his Aunt Jane, whom "I now began to know and, what was the same thing, to love".

This one visit to Southampton left an enduring picture in young Edward's mind.

> My grandmother's house had a pleasant garden, bordered on one side by the old city wall; the top of this wall was sufficiently wide to afford a pleasant walk, with an exterior view, easily accessible to the ladies. This must have been a part of the identical walls which witnessed the embarkation of Henry V before the Battle of Agincourt.

Even more fascinating to the little boy must have been the extraordinary castellated mansion belonging to the Marquis of Lansdowne, which stood in Castle Square, blocking the view from the windows on that side of the house, but affording a glimpse of something even more delightful. Every day the child would station himself at one of the windows to see the Marchioness's phaeton and ponies being assembled.

The Marchioness had a light phaeton, drawn by six, and sometimes by eight little ponies, each pair decreasing in size, and becoming lighter in colour, through all the grades of dark brown, light brown, bay and chestnut, as it was placed farther away from the carriage. The two leading ponies were managed by boyish postillions, the two pairs nearest were driven by hand. It was a delight to me to look down from the window and see this fairy equipage put together; for the precincts of this castle were so contracted that the whole process went on in the little space that remained of the open square.

Edward's little sister, Caroline, who soon grew to love her Aunt Jane as well as he did, never visited the house at Southampton, but his step-sister, Anna, stayed there when the rest of the family were at Godmersham. Anna was at that time a delightful, moody, difficult fifteen-year-old who adored her aunts and completely baffled her step-mother. It was typical of her to insist on cropping her hair short in the latest fashion, and her aunts could only console themselves by assuring each other that it would surely grow again before long. It was a little unfortunate for Anna that her cousin Fanny at Godmersham was becoming the perfect niece – "almost another sister", as her Aunt Jane said. Doubtless Fanny would never have dreamed of recklessly cutting off her hair.

Fanny was to have her own special problems before long. During that memorable family party at Godmersham, Jane had noticed that her sister-in-law Elizabeth was looking a little tired and unwell. She was then pregnant with her eleventh child, and some weeks after the party had dispersed, Cassandra set out as usual for Godmersham to stay with her brother and sister-in-law for the birth, and the long convalescence customary in those days. It would have been unthinkable in that particular family to welcome a new baby without Cassandra's help. On the first of October she wrote to her mother and Jane with the good news that all was safely over; the baby had been born just before she arrived and mother and son were doing well. Little Brook John continued to thrive, but his mother's apparently swift recovery had been illusory; in less than a fornight she became seriously ill and died very suddenly, leaving behind her a husband distraught with grief and eleven motherless children.

The two eldest boys, Edward and George, were at Winchester College, and James went over to break the news to them and bring them home – not to Godmersham, which was considered too far, but to Steventon. After a brief stay they were sent on by coach to Southampton, where they arrived chilled to the bone after travelling without their greatcoats. The coachman did his best to make up for the deficiency by spreading the folds of his own voluminous many-caped garment to cover them a little, but the lads were numb with cold when for the first time, in such sad circumstances, they set foot in Castle Square.

The boys were not only numb with cold; they were numb with shock. For a young boy or girl such an experience is traumatic. Afterwards it is remembered as something set apart from time, especially if absence from home is involved. Edward and George had said goodbye to their dearly loved mother when setting out for school, but already the recollection was indistinct; they had been excited about the return to school and about seeing their friends again. It had never occurred to them that they might never see their mother again. They longed for home but were told the journey would be too far; they longed for one last sight of her lovely face, at the same time dreading it, only to find that this must be denied them. The brief stay with Uncle and Aunt James was already a confused memory of well-meaning attempts at consolation, and the company of cousins too young to understand – except for Anna, and she was only a girl. Mourning clothes had been ordered, but they were not suitable, in their opinion, and they could not explain what was wrong. Then suddenly they were with Aunt Jane and everything seemed different. Yes, of course they must have their proper mourning clothes and yes, of course they must be like the ones other boys wore when they were bereaved. Nobody critized them when they burst into tears over a letter from their father; it was perfectly natural and only to be expected, but when they had dried their eyes, perhaps they would like to take a stroll with Aunt Jane and have a look at the river. When they were indoors, out came the ivory spillikins, or a pack of cards, or cup-and-ball; they were never at a loss for something to do. On the other hand, they were not prevented from giving way to their grief; Edward nearly broke down in church on the Sunday morning, but afterwards Aunt Jane took them down to the quay where there was plenty to interest them. George even boarded a collier in his Sunday clothes without being scolded for it. Afterwards the boys would remember the old house in Southampton as a place where the saddest hours of their young lives had been unaccountably happy ones.

Edward Austen Leigh, James and Mary's son, in the memoir he wrote about his aunt, described her as having had two homes, Steventon and Chawton. In Bath and Southampton, he said, "she was only a sojourner in a strange land". It seems as if of all her nephews and nieces, and in spite of the appearance to the contrary given by both Cassandra and Jane in their preference for Fanny, James's children understood her best. Wayward, tomboyish Anna, Edward the would-be writer, and little Caroline, who was only twelve when she died, all have the same touch and they kept it to the end of their lives. Fanny, dear, loving, pretty little Fanny, with all her delightful love affairs, would eventually become an aristocratic lady and recall her "provincial" aunts, not only with love and admiration, but with a certain embarrassment; it would be left to Anna, Edward and Caroline to keep to the core of the matter.

Edward was right in referring to Chawton as Jane's second home. Steventon inspired the *Juvenilia* and the early drafts of her first three novels; Chawton saw the full flowering of her genius; Bath and Southampton, like Number 1 Paragon, always seemed "dark" in comparison, and all they produced was the revised *Lady Susan*, finally to be put aside, and the first chapters of *The Watsons*, never to be completed, but which in other circumstances might well have been brought to fruition later on in Chawton.

Jane's brother, Edward, had decided to leave Godmersham temporally and take up residence in his other great house at Chawton. Henceforth he and his family would be using both their lovely homes intermittently. Meanwhile he had decided that it was time to do something more for his mother and sisters. Frank's scheme for establishing his wife, his mother, his sisters and Martha Lloyd in that roomy old house in Southampton had worked surprisingly well, but it could not go on for ever. Frank and Mary's first baby, Mary Jane, was born in 1808, and doubtless they were well on the way to establishing a family. Mrs Austen was already thinking of moving to fresh quarters when Edward's timely offer arrived. Two small houses were at his disposal, one at Godmersham and one at Chawton. Which would she prefer? Mrs Austen had no doubts in the matter and neither had her daughters. Hampshire was "home" to her rather than Kent, and at Chawton they would be within comparatively easy reach of Steventon. Provided that the house at Chawton was large enough for the four of them, with room to spare for guests, and especially for family, including grandchildren, Chawton it must be.

A timely letter from Henry reassured his mother about the size of the house; it had six bedrooms, not including useful garrets for storage, and so was admirably suited to their needs. Edward was generous in his offers of help; he would make any alterations they required for their comfort and help them in every possible way. From now on Jane's letters to Cassandra are full of plans for their new home. Yes, they would have a manservant and one of the garrets could be fitted up for his use – "his name shall be Robert if you please," added Jane. And they must have a piano again, "as good a one as can be got for thirty guineas," and Jane would play country dances for their nephews and nieces. Mrs Knight, Edward's widowed adoptive mother, had suggested that it would be an admirable plan for Jane to marry the vicar, Mr Papillon; "she may depend upon it but I *will* marry Mr. Papillon," wrote Jane, "whatever may be his reluctance or my own. I owe her more than such a trifling sacrifice." Jane was obviously in tearing high spirits. The very thought of the house at Chawton set her heart dancing. She knew that she was coming home.

10

THE HOUSE AT CHAWTON was "home", as soon as they moved into it. Jane must have felt like a little cat with its paws well buttered, for she settled in at once, and within a few days was writing doggerel verses to Frank at sea:

> Cassandra's pen will paint our state,
> The many comforts that await
> Our Chawton home, how much we find
> Already in it, to our mind;
> And how convinced, that when complete
> It will all other houses beat
> That ever have been made or mended,
> With rooms concise or rooms distended.

The lines were part of a long string of verses written to congratulate Frank on the birth of his little son.

> My dearest Frank, I wish you joy
> Of Mary's safety with a boy,
> Whose birth has given little pain
> Compared with that of Mary Jane —
> May he a growing Blessing prove
> And well deserve his Parents Love;

It seems strange that Jane should ever have tried her hand at verse; even her serious lament for Mrs Lefroy is a sadly pedestrian effort. Her mother had a neater hand for doggerel and probably knew it. Perhaps that explains why it was a long time before she recognized her daughter's genius. Possibly she never did. Certainly, lively old lady that she was, she could spoil even *Pride and Prejudice* by reading it aloud in such a way as to make it a dull recital.

There was no dressing room attached to the sisters' small bedroom at Chawton, to make a sitting room or a writing room for them. If Jane wanted to take up her writing again, she must do so in the common parlour, where she would be liable to interruptions of every kind. This would have mattered at Bath or Southampton, where she either had no will to write because she was unhappy, or was unhappy because she had no real will to write. Here at Chawton it could make no difference; this small mellow house with its welcoming atmosphere was home. The interruptions presented no problem; the parlour door creaked and Jane would not have it altered. She wrote in secret, and the warning creak enabled her to slip her work under the blotting paper before the uninvited guest stepped inside. Moreover, she had long accustomed herself to deal with interruptions, whether in the course of her work or in the course of her life. She had achieved that inward discipline which enables the writer to come to terms with interruptions of all kinds, treating them as a contribution rather than an impoverishment to life. Afterwards, she was able to take up her work again where she had left it and find that the life was still in it.

Jane Austen was a perfectionist. Her first impulse was to take out one of her manuscripts and give it the final revision she considered to be necessary. It could not be *Susan*; she had tried to retrieve the manuscript before leaving Southampton, but nothing except the repayment of the ten pounds would persuade Mr Crosby to return it, and Jane could not easily afford such a sum. Morever, a novel was published that year with the title *Susan*; if ever she was able to retrieve the manuscript she would have to change the title, and possibly also the heroine's name. There were too many complications; *Susan* had better stay where she was, at least for the time being. It could not be *First Impressions*; this was Jane's favourite and she could not bear the thought of another rejection. It would have to be *Elinor and Marianne*, now retitled *Sense and Sensibility*; she had enough faith in it to undertake the revision, but it would never be flesh of her flesh and bone of her bone as *First Impressions* was.

Again Jane consulted her brother Henry, and again Henry entered into the affair with enthusiasm. Thomas Egerton of the Military Library, Whitehall, was prepared to undertake the publication, but he would take no risks; Jane must be prepared to reimburse him for any loss incurred. Encouraged by Henry, Jane was willing to risk it; she set aside a sum of money and hoped it would be enough. The novel was to be published anonymously with simply "by a Lady" on the title page; the last thing Jane wanted was to draw attention to herself. Henry was delighted by his success at finding a publisher, and he and Eliza warmly invited Jane to come and stay with them in London, so that she could be in close touch with Mr Egerton and correct at least some of the proofs on the spot.

Henry and Eliza were at that time living in a large, comfortable house in Sloane Street; their previous home had been in the pleasant little village of Brompton, and Jane had once stayed with them there on her way to Godmersham. Now Henry and Eliza were going up in the world; Henry was a successful banker in the firm of Austen, Maude and Tilson, and the mansion in Sloane Street was next door to that of his partner, Mr Tilson. Eliza was a charming hostess and the house was ideal for entertaining. Soon after Jane's arrival they held a musical party to which they invited eighty guests; like many hostesses of today Eliza expected only about half of them to turn up, but at least sixty accepted and the drawing rooms were well filled, and too hot for Jane's liking. She took refuge in the passage connecting the two rooms, where she was well pleased to hear the music and not be too hemmed in by the company. She remarked wryly in a letter to Cassandra that "the Performers gave great satisfaction by doing what they were paid for, and giving themselves no airs – no amateurs could be persauded to do anything". Obviously Jane enjoyed the programme, but she had a great mistrust of people who went into ecstasies over music, or pretended to have more knowledge of it than they possessed. She herself was the most musical member of an unmusical family; she could play the piano well enough to accompany simple dancing, and she could also sing in a very pretty voice, but gushing ladies who *doted* on music were anathema to her. Actually she was more knowledgeable on the subject than she pretended to be. In a reference to Anna in the same letter, she described the young girl as "quite an Anna with variations – but she cannot have reached her last, for that is always the most flourishing and shewey – she is at about her 3rd or 4th, which are generally simple and pretty". However many variations there might be to Anna's theme song, one characteristic never wavered, and that was her devotion to her Aunt Jane.

In all the excitement of her stay at Sloane Street, with the party, and shopping expeditions, and visits to the theatre – though she missed seeing Mrs Siddons, to her great regret – Jane did not overlook the main reason for her journey. "No, indeed," she wrote in answer to a query from Cassandra, "I am never too busy to think of S and S. I can no more forget it than a mother could her sucking child; and I am much obliged to you for your enquiries. I have had two sheets to correct, but the last only brings us to W's first appearance. Mrs. K [Edward's adoptive mother] regrets in the most

115

flattering manner that she must wait *till* May, but I have scarcely a hope of its being out in June. – Henry does not neglect it; he *has* hurried the Printer, and says he will see him again today."

Jane was right in her expectations of delay, and poor Mrs Knight had to wait until October, when at last the three volumes of *Sense and Sensibility* appeared at the booksellers and on the shelves of the circulating libraries. Even the little circulating library at Alton had copies. Anna saw them on the counter one day, when she had walked in to Alton with her Aunt Jane. Noticing this new publication, she picked up the first volume to look at it more closely. "*Sense and Sensibility!*" she exclaimed. "Well, Aunt, you can tell it must be rubbish from the title!" Aunt Jane did not enlighten her. She preferred to keep the secret, even from the younger members of her own family, at least for the time being.

If only Anna had read as far as the second chapter, she would have been swept into the book as so many readers were. The second chapter of *Sense and Sensibility* must be amongst the most brilliant and witty early chapters in literature, with John Dashwood discussing with his wife what he ought to do to fulfil the promise made to his dying father, to look after his step-mother and his step-sisters. Ought he to give his sisters a thousand pounds apiece? Why, what would they do with such a sum? And how wrong it would be to impoverish the estate which his own little son would inherit. Oh no, his father cannot possibly have meant anything like that! And so gradually any generous intentions he may have had are whittled down, until the couple agree that they are being very generous in helping with the removal and sending the family an occasional present of fish or game when in season.

There was no need for Jane to draw on the sum she had put by, so that she could reimburse the publisher for any loss. The book went well; in two years every copy had been sold and Jane had made a profit of a hundred and forty pounds. Meanwhile, the sooner this success could be followed up by another publication, the better. Jane had started on a new story, but with her meticulous care in revision this might take her some time. Surely now she could risk taking out the manuscript of *First Impressions*. She knew in her heart that it was a better book, but she also knew that another rejection would be too hard to bear. Eventually she took it out and began to revise it again. She also changed the title. *Sense and Sensibility* had proved attractive to the general public; this should be another alliterative and revealing title: *Pride and Prejudice*. It is believed that this particular title came from the closing line of Fanny Burney's *Cecilia*, where the words PRIDE and PREJU-DICE are thrice repeated, printed in capital letters. There was no question of a second refusal. Jane did not even have to publish the book at her own risk. Mr Egerton bought it outright for a hundred and ten pounds, and one cannot but suspect that he knew this was a bargain.

Of all Jane's novels, she cared most intensely about this one and about its heroine – "I must confess that I think her as delightful a creature as ever appeared in print," she wrote to Cassandra "and how I shall be able to tolerate those who do not like *her* at least, I do not know." From that day to this, readers have fallen in love with Elizabeth Bennet and, to a lesser extent, with her gentle sister, Jane; few have paused to ask how such an apparently ill-matched pair as Mr and Mrs Bennet managed to produce, in the first instance, two such enchanting daughters, only to be followed by three such silly ones, though doubtless stranger things have happened. The book sparkles from beginning to end and the characters are all alive to their fingertips. At last Jane can give vent to her anti-snob complex with the immortal Lady Catherine de Bourgh, and she manages to pierce those countless bubbles of fashionable musical pretension at the same time; "It is of all subjects my delight. I must have my share in the conversation if you are speaking of music. There are few people in England, I suppose, who have more true enjoyment of music than myself, or a better musical taste. If I had ever learnt I should have been a great Proficient."

Jane can depict a *pseudo* gentleman who is a rogue, and a London tradesman and his wife who are in the truest sense of the word gentlefolk; she can bring alive in one of her characters the agonies of shyness which she knew as a little girl, and she can shew in an adult male character how just such shyness, if suppressed, can result in apparent haughtiness and pride. She can encourage sympathy and support for Elizabeth's refusal of the egregious Mr Collins, but she can also make the sensible Charlotte's decision to marry him for the sake of an establishment credible, and to some extent laudable.

"Upon the whole, however," wrote Jane to Cassandra, "I am quite vain enough and well satisfied enough. The work is rather too light, and bright, and sparkling; it wants shade; it wants to be stretched out here and there with a long chapter of sense, if it could be had; if not, of some solemn specious nonsense, about something unconnected with the story: an essay on writing, a critique on Walter Scott, or the history of Buonaparte, or anything that will form a contrast, and bring the reader with increased delight to the playfulness and epigrammatism of the general style." It wanted, of course, nothing of the kind, and Jane and Cassandra knew it. So did Henry, though he was in no mood for lightheartedness at the time. His darling Eliza was already showing signs of the fatal illness which was to part her from him a few months later.

Pride and Prejudice was published early in 1813 and already the next book was taking shape. Jane insisted that it would involve a complete change of subject. It would be about ordination. So it was, but how much more besides! Homesickness enters into it, with such a vivid description of little Fanny sobbing on the stairs that one is tempted to wonder if little Jane had sobbed on the stairs at Mrs Cawley's. Fanny, adopted by her wealthy relations, has everything heart could desire except the one place for which her heart is aching, like "the sad heart of Ruth, when sick for home, She stood in tears amid the alien corn". Unrequited love enters into the story; Fanny goes on loving Edmund against all reason or probability, and she would have gone on loving him for the rest of her life with no return – and gaining no sympathy from the attention of some modern readers of *Mansfield Park*. People who sit "Like Patience on a monument, Smiling at grief " can expect little sympathy today. The Crawfords of this world will get such sympathy as may be available; they are lively, intelligent, attractive young people who will take all that is offered to them and more besides. Incidentally, one of the fascinating things about Henry Crawford is that, as Lord David Cecil once pointed out, he came alive so strongly as to be beyond the control of his creator. She managed to wrench him back into his nefarious role, but there was a price to be paid and that price had to be paid by Fanny.

There was a family tradition that Mary Crawford was modelled on Eliza de Feuillide, which is hard to believe, since Eliza was dying as the story came to life in Jane's mind. Probably there was nothing conscious about it – Jane loathed it when people suggested that any of her characters were exactly drawn from life. It seems more likely that Mary Crawford embodied the childhood memory of the lovely, fascinating young girl who was kind to her shy little cousin and stuck up for her when she was criticized.

Nobody seems to have a good word to say about Mrs Norris – "detestable" "disagreeable," are the adjectives commonly used by critics. Yet she is alive and consistent from the beginning to the end of the book, active in other people's business, keeping dependants and poor relations in their place, and always with a sharp eye to her own advantage, so that the offending stage curtains are whisked away to her cottage, where she happens to be "particularly in want of green baize", and she returns from that ill-fated visit to Southerton the happiest member of the party, with the rare plant coaxed from the gardener, and the parcel of cheese, and the pheasant's eggs which she has wheedled out of the housekeeper, who will "take no denial". She plans to get the dairymaid at Mansfield Park "to sit them under the first spare hen, and if they come to good I can have them moved to my own house and borrow a coop". That coop is far more likely to be kept in the poultry yard at Mansfield Park, where somebody else can look after it. Mrs Norris is not detestable, however much she bullies poor Fanny; we all know her, we all enjoy wondering what on earth she will get up to next; she is only a little trying if she happens to be one's own aunt.

Eliza died in April after a long and painful illness, from which there could be no hope of recovery. Henry seemed inconsolable, but as Jane said later on in a letter to Francis in July, "his Mind is not a Mind for affliction, he is too busy, too active, too sanguine". Meanwhile Jane paid a visit to Sloane Street in May; Henry came over in his curricle to stay at Chawton and take his sister home with him. He was full of plans to move from Sloane Street, where alas! there was now no lovely hostess to entertain their friends, and to organize those delightful musical parties, to rooms above the offices of Tilson's Bank in Henrietta Street. Jane entered into all his arrangements and plans with enthusiasm. He did not think he would be settled there until the late Autumn – "he 'will not be come to bide' till after September," she wrote to Cassandra, quoting a childish saying of Frank's which had become part of the family tradition. In spite of the sad circumstances, Jane enjoyed her visit. Henry took her to see some of the spring exhibitions of pictures; at one in Spring Gardens, she saw a small portrait which she identified at once as resembling Mrs Bingley, née Bennet, from

Pride and Prejudice – it was excessively like her, she said. But nowhere could she find one of Mrs Darcy. "I am disappointed," she told her sister. "I can only imagine that Mr. D prizes any picture of her too much to like it should be exposed to the public eye – I can imagine he would have that sort of feeling – that mixture of Love, Pride and Delicacy."

Doubtless Henry must have derived amusement as well as comfort from Jane's visit. He could not do enough for her. Jane, for her part, appreciated both the quiet she enjoyed when he was out on business, and the amusements he planned for her, especially the drives in his barouche – "I liked my solitary elegance very much, and was ready to laugh all the time, at my being where I was. – I could not but feel that I had naturally small right to be parading about London in a Barouche."

Jane finished *Mansfield Park* in July, having checked every detail in the meticulous way which was customary with her. So far as is known, she only slipped up once, and that was in *Emma*, when she described the view from Donwell Abbey which was so admired by some of the guests at Mr Knightley's strawberry party. She referred to "orchards in blossom", greatly to the amusement of her brother Edward, who was the first to notice the error. "I should like to know, Jane, where you got those apple trees of yours that blossom in July?" he enquired.

The greater part of *Mansfield Park* was set in Northamptonshire, a county which was unfamiliar to her, but she was careful to make the necessary enquiries. She had chosen Northamptonshire because she needed good hunting country to account for the Crawfords' repeated visits to the Grants, and also because her scene of action needed to be well removed from Portsmouth, so that Fanny might indeed feel cut off from her home and family. Fanny's elder brother, William, was to go to sea very early in the story, and here she needed Frank's advice, and his permission to use the names of some of his former ships. William may have been a comparatively minor character, but the details of his career were very clearly in her mind. As for the delightful young William Price himself, nothing will ever prevent her readers from identifying him with her "own particular little brother", Charles.

It was not long before Jane stayed with Henry again, this time with a large contingent of the Edward Austens, now known as the Knights. When Mrs Knight, Edward's adoptive mother, died in 1812, he changed his name to Knight, and his sister Jane said resignedly: "I must learn to make a better K." Jane was delighted with 10 Henrietta Street; so much of the Sloane Street furniture had been moved into it that she felt quite at home there. Henrietta Street is a small street leading to Covent Garden market; in those days it must have been busy with country folk bringing their wares into the town. Exactly opposite the house is the passage leading to St Paul's Church, now known as the Actors' Church. In Jane Austen's day, this church would have been fairly recently rebuilt, after a disastrous fire in 1795; it was faithfully restored in accordance with the original plan, which was by Inigo Jones. It is said that Inigo Jones's instructions from his cheese-paring patron were to build a church like a barn. "Then, sir," said the architect, "it will be the handsomest barn in Europe." Incidentally, it was in the portico of St Paul's Church, Covent Garden, that Bernard Shaw's Henry Higgins first met the flower girl, Eliza Dolittle.

Fanny, Lizzie and Marianne were all included in this family visit, and their programme varied from the delights of Don Juan, "whom we left in Hell at half-past-eleven," said their aunt, to the horrors of the dentist, which "cost us many tears". Sympathetic Aunt Jane took a poor view of the dentist; "I would not have him look at mine for a shilling a tooth and double it," she wrote afterwards.

The nieces evidently had fun modernizing their aunt's hair style, for they carried her off to the opera with her hair curled and no cap – "only a bit of velvet round my head". It was on this occasion that Jane expressed much disappointment on seeing nothing of Mr Crabbe; she was a great admirer of Crabbe's poetry and used to say jokingly that if she had ever married, she could have fancied being Mrs Crabbe.

Afterwards, when they were all at Godmersham, Cassandra mentioned in one of her letters that she had seen an announcement of the death of the real Mrs Crabbe. "Poor woman!" wrote Jane. "I will comfort *him* as well as I can, but I do not undertake to be good to her children. She had better not leave any."

It was four years since she had stayed at Godmersham, and this was to be a long visit. While she was there, she heard of Anna's engagement to Ben Lefroy, the youngest son of her dear friend, Madame Lefroy. Poor Anna had a mercurial temperament and was often the despair of her staid father and her stepmother. She had already been engaged for a short time to a Mr Michael Terry, for no better reason, apparently, than that she had been missing her stepbrother, Edward, after his return to Winchester. It was difficult to tell which caused her parents to be most upset, the original engagement or its cancellation. This second engagement proved to be a more hopeful affair, though the young couple experienced a good many ups and downs before they were married in the following year. "I have had a late account from Steventon," wrote Jane to Cassandra, "and a baddish one so far as Ben is concerned. He has declined a curacy (apparently highly eligible) which he might have secured against his taking Orders, and upon its being made such a serious question, says he has not made up his mind as to taking Orders so early, and that if his father makes a point of it, he must give Anna up rather than do what he does not approve. He must be maddish. They are going on again at present as before – but it cannot last." It seemed that Anna was not the only one of the young couple who could be described as an Anna – or a Ben – "with variations".

II

M ANSFIELD PARK" was published in May, 1814, and the first
edition was sold out by the autumn. Henry had been enthusiastic about it in manuscript; Jane read part of it to him
when they were travelling together from Chawton to London, early in
March. "Henry's approbation hitherto is even equal to my
wishes," wrote Jane to Cassandra, and she added that he thought it
very different from the other two, but not at all inferior. He finished it later and found the last part "extremely interesting". He
was in some doubt as to how the plot was going to work out,
whether "HC would be reformed or would forget Fanny in a fort-
night".

Henry's approbation meant a great deal to his sister; she could
almost forgive him for occasionally betraying the secret of her
authorship, though she still preferred to guard this from the outside
world, largely owing to her unconquerable shyness. The lively,
witty Miss Jane Austen of former days, who seldom lacked partners in the ballroom and could dance tirelessly and radiantly into
the small hours, does not give the lie to this statement; Jane could
and did act a part to perfection, and she derived a great deal of exquisite enjoyment from so doing, but basically she was shy. This
accounts for some of the criticism she received from her contemporaries. For example, Mary Russell Mitford, daughter of her

former critic, Mrs Mitford, and an enthusiastic admirer of her work, passed on a formidable description of her, which she had received from a friend. "A friend of mine, who visits her now, says that she has stiffened into the most perpendicular, precise, taciturn piece of single blessedness that ever existed, and that, till *Pride and Prejudice* showed what a precious gem was hidden in that unbending case, she was no more regarded in society than a poker or a firescreen, or any other thin or upright piece of wood that fills its corner in peace and quietness. The case is very different now; she is still a poker – but a poker of whom everyone is afraid. It must be confessed that this silent observation from such an observer is rather formidable. Most writers are good-humoured chatterers. But a wit, a delineator of character who does not talk, is terrific indeed. After all, I do not know that I can quite vouch for this account."

Mary Russell Mitford was right in doubting whether she could vouch for this account, especially as her friend happened to be one of a family involved in a vindictive lawsuit with Edward (Austen) Knight. In any case, silence in company is a typical attribute of extreme shyness, and Jane was not the only author to suffer from it. One is increasingly reminded of Charlotte Brontë's contribution to the conversation at Thackeray's famous dinner party. "Do you like London, Miss Brontë?" – prolonged pause – "Yes and no."

The visit to Henrietta Street in March was to be the last, though not the least enjoyable. It was a bitter winter and the snow lay thick on the ground, but Henry's quarters were snug and warm. While Jane was there, Edward and his daughter, Fanny, joined them and they all went to see Edmund Kean as Shylock, which was an unforgettable experience. Jane could find no fault with his performance and longed to see him act again.

When next Jane visited Henry in London, he had moved to 23 Hans Place, a large mansion not far from his former home in

Sloane Street. She liked her brother's new home much better than she had expected. "I find more space and comfort in the rooms than I had supposed, and the garden is quite a love." She had the nicest bedroom in the house, on an upper floor with a wide view of the neighbouring houses and gardens. This was still a comparatively rural area, with cows being herded along the narrow lanes to the farm, and a pleasant prospect of green fields.

Jane was already at work on another book. She had begun it in January, during the bitterly cold weather, and her early comment is revealing: "I am going to take a heroine whom no-one but myself will much like." Emma is a spoilt, charming, opinionated young girl, redeemed from the very first by her tender care of her hypochondriacal semi-invalid father. Their home is entirely centred in him; every whim must be attended to, and nobody ever seems to have given Emma any credit for her skill and tact as a youthful housekeeper. These must have been considerable or Serle, the cook, for example, would surely have given notice when the appetizing delicacies so carefully prepared for Mr Woodhouse and his friends were rejected as unwholesome. It would have been no comfort to Serle to overhear Mr Woodhouse's assurance to his guests: "Serle understands boiling an egg better than anybody."

Through *Emma*, Jane Austen worked out, consciously or unconsciously, her feelings about snobbery. Emma, in her unconscionable meddling with other people's lives, does not scruple to use the weapon of snobbery to gain her ends – for their own good, of course. "It would have grieved me to lose your acquaintance, which must have been the consequence of your marrying Mr Martin," she said to Harriet, her protegée. Robert Martin is a respectable young farmer, but she considers him to be of precisely the order of people with whom she can have nothing to do. By the end of the story, the news of Harriet's engagement to Robert

Martin delights her, to the astonishment of Mr Knightley, to whom she herself is now engaged. He feels her attitude must have changed considerably since last they discussed this subject, and so it has. Emma has grown up.

In a sense, *Emma* is all about the painful process of growing up. In a deeper sense, it is about growing in grace. "Grow in grace," says the concluding passage of the Second General Epistle of Peter, and we tend to take it at its face value, like "Have a good time!" or "Safe journey!" or "Enjoy yourself!" Growing in grace is not an easy, fool-proof recipe for Instant Happiness. Somewhere along the line there is bound to be a confrontation, as Emma found in her humiliation and mortification after she had been rude to Miss Bates. "How could she have been so brutal, so cruel to Miss Bates!" She could have bitten her tongue out. She would have given anything to have another chance, to be able to take the words back and begin again. Nobody could have told her that this was to be a growing point, and if they had, she would not have believed them. But "out of this nettle, danger, We pluck this flower, safety". Only the safety is not of this world; it is the inward core of self-discipline.

Miss Bates is one of God's fools, one of those characters of whom G. K. Chesterton wrote: "The great fool is above wisdom rather than below it." Sir Arthur Quiller-Couch pursued the theme in his Cambridge lectures on Dickens. "But, like Charles Lamb, Jane Austen and Dickens both 'loved a fool': Jane delicately, Dickens riotously: witness the one's Miss Bates, the other's Mr. Toots. But observe, pray, the fools they delight in are always – like Slender, like Miss Bates, like Mr. Toots – simple fools, sincere fools, good at heart, good to live with, and in their way, the salt of the earth. Miss Bates herself bears unconscious witness to this in one of her wisest foolishest remarks – 'it is such a happiness when good people get together – and they always do.'" Jane Austen had outgrown, not only her early, surface mockery of female eccentricity, but also the compassionate attitude implied in "Poor Mrs. Stent! It has been her lot to be always in the way." She had entered into the company of the initiates in recognizing God's fools as the salt of the earth. "What are commonly the world's received fools," asked Charles Lamb, "but such whereof the world is not worthy?"

Even as Jane was living herself into the world of *Emma*, another claim was made upon her time. Anna had embarked upon a novel, and had begun to send off the earlier chapters to her Aunt Jane for criticism. Considering the attitude of most authors to unsolicited manuscripts, it is amazing that Jane was able to write: "I am very much obliged to you for sending your MS." She and her mother and Cassandra all read it and were pleased with it, but only Jane could give it the detailed attention it needed. The original title was *Enthusiasm*, but at an early stage Anna changed it to *Which is the Heroine?*, which sounds like something by Anthony Trollope. Rather surprisingly, Jane preferred the earlier title, but she thought she might take to the second one in time.

One of Jane's most lovable attributes was that she never "talked down" to children, or to young people with literary aspirations. She went into every detail of Anna's manuscript, always following up criticism with praise, in consideration for the feelings of the young author. When little Caroline, Anna's stepsister, produced a manuscript for criticism, her Aunt Jane, who was busy with her own work at the time, wrote to her at once:

My dear Caroline,
    I wish I could finish stories as fast as you can. – I am much obliged to you for the sight of Olivia, and think you have done for her very well, but the good-for-nothing Father who was the real author of all her Faults and Sufferings,

should not escape punishment. I hope *he* hung himself, or took the surname of *Bone* or underwent some dreadful penance or other.

Your affectionate J. Austen.

In one of her letters to Anna, which is full of constructive and detailed criticism, she not only gives praise when it is due, but treats her as a fellow-author: "You are now collecting your People delightfully, getting them exactly into such a spot as is the delight of my life; — 3 or 4 Families in a Country Village is the very thing to work on." This letter was interrupted by tragic news from the Nore: Charles's wife had died in childbirth, leaving three motherless little girls. The eldest, Cassy, "that puss Cass", as Jane called her, had often stayed at Chawton, evoking another aspect of Jane's sympathetic understanding of children. Cassy was apt to be criticized for being unresponsive, but her Aunt Jane was always ready to give her time. The little girl did not wear her heart on her sleeve, but behind her shyness and awkwardness, she was a very lovable child. Perhaps Cassy was all too aware that her younger sister, Harriet, was thought to be "a truly sweet-tempered little Darling". When the sad news arrived, Jane added a note to Anna's letter, explaining what had happened, but still encouraging her to send further instalments of her story when they were ready, though she would not be able to read them aloud to Mrs Austen until the old lady had recovered from the shock.

This correspondence continued for over a year, and in the course of it, Anna was married to Ben Lefroy at Steventon Church. The first months of their married life were spent at Hendon, and Jane and her brother Edward visited them there one day, when they were staying at Hans Place. Jane was inclined to be critical. Anna had bought a purple pelisse, which her aunt thought was extravagant of her when she did not really need it, and the young couple had ordered a piano for twenty-four guineas when they should have been buying more sheets and towels. Probably Jane was harking back to her own youth, when she seldom had any money to spare. This mood did not last long; within a month she was teasing Anna about the latest instalment of her book. "It is very well told – and his having been in love with the Aunt gives Cecilia additional Interest with him. I like the Idea: – A very proper compliment to an aunt! – I rather imagine that Neices are seldom chosen but in compliment to some Aunt. I daresay Ben was in love with me once, and would never have thought of *you* if he had not supposed me dead of a scarlet fever."

Later, in 1815, Ben and Anna Lefroy moved to a house called Wyards, near Alton, where their first child, Anna Jemima, was born. The manuscript was laid aside for the time being. Anna's life was now full and busy; some day she would take it out again and continue the story. But when that day came, Anna, with tears in her eyes, consigned the manuscript to the flames, and one of her little girls sat on the hearth by her side and watched the sparks flying up the chimney. Anna could not bear to finish it, now that her Aunt Jane was no more.

Fanny did not write stories for her aunt to criticize. She did something which may have been even better; she consulted her about her love affairs. Fanny was not only motherless; she had no special sister to confide in, for the members of the family nearest to her in age were all boys. Poor Fanny poured out her troubles in long letters to her Aunt Jane, letters which must on no account be shared with Aunt Cassandra. All the nephews and nieces knew that Aunt Cassandra and Aunt Jane were absolutely trustworthy in this respect. Secrets shared with one of them would never be passed on to the other without permission. Jane showed extraordinary wisdom in guiding her beloved niece during this period. "Oh! dear Fanny," she wrote at one point, when an attachment seemed to be cooling off, "your mistake has been one that thousands of women fall into. He was the *first* young man who attached himself to you." Unlike her own Lady Russell in *Persuasion*, Jane would never actively interfere. "You frightened me out of my wits by your reference," she writes. "Your affection gives me the highest pleasure, but indeed you must not let anything depend on my opinion. Your own feelings and none but your own, should determine such an important point."

Emma was finished in March, 1815, but doubtless the manuscript had to be subjected to a final revision before Jane went to stay with Henry at Hans Place in the autumn, for negotiations with the publisher. This time she decided to make a change. Mr Egerton had declined to reprint *Mansfield Park*, and Henry was negotiating with the famous publishing house of John Murray for *Emma*, and for the copyrights of *Mansfield Park* and *Sense and Sensibility*. The terms offered were somewhat disappointing, and one wonders if Henry was quite the expert business man his family believed him to be. On the other hand, he had business worries of his own, as most bankers had in that fateful year, and he was not in good health at the time. While Jane was staying with him, he had a severe bilious attack, with a touch of fever. He had been subject to bilious attacks for some time. "Dearest Henry!" wrote Jane once to Cassandra. "What a turn he has for being ill!"

Henry stayed in bed, but this time the trouble did not clear up. Jane sent for the apothecary, a clever young man called Mr Haydon, and he prescribed treatment which seemed to do the patient some good. His sister had begun to hope for a complete and early recovery, when suddenly Henry had a serious relapse which alarmed her so much that she sent for Cassandra, James and Edward, who all came at once, Edward bringing Fanny with him. For an agonizing week, Henry seemed to be hovering between life and death, and only his sister's devoted nursing pulled him through.

132

Though the dangerous stage of his illness only lasted for a week, Henry continued to be in very indifferent health for some time. Probably his business worries militated against his recovery. Jane stayed on, and so did Fanny; kind Mr Haydon was a frequent visitor, both to the patient and to the patient's relatives; he was a lover of music and so was Fanny, and they all spent some pleasant evenings together. "We really grow so fond of Mr. Haydon that I do not know what to expect," wrote Jane to Cassandra. Cassandra seems to have had her own ideas about what to expect; it was not long before Edward returned to Hans Place and took his daughter home.

One interesting result followed from the friendship with Mr Haydon. Mr Haydon knew one of the Prince Regent's physicians, and it is believed that he brought him in for a consultation. The secret of Jane's authorship could not possibly be kept under Henry's roof, and so it came about that the Prince Regent, who was a great admirer of the novels, was told that Miss Jane Austen was in town, and that she was the author of the works he so enjoyed. As a result, the Prince's Librarian, Mr Clarke, was instructed to call upon her and to invite her to inspect the library at Carlton House.

Jane Austen was no admirer of the Prince Regent. In the general dispute over his matrimonial difficulties, her sympathies were on the side of the Princess – "Poor Woman, I shall support her as long as I can, because she *is* a Woman and because I hate her husband." However, she was not inclined to reject this mark of favour, especially as she was told that the Prince Regent was so great an admirer of her work that he kept a set of her novels in each of his residences. His brother, the Duke of York, and his daughter, Princess Charlotte, also enjoyed reading them. Jane Austen duly visited the library at Carlton House and, judging by Mr Clarke's subsequent letters, one might guess that she had little opportunity to make any observations on its treasures. Indeed, Mr Clarke paid her so many "flattering attentions", that she came away in some doubt as to what he had actually said. Had he really informed her that she had His Royal Highness's permission to dedicate her next or some future book to him? She was so confused about this that she wrote tactfully to ask Mr Clarke what this permission really implied. Mr Clarke was delighted, not only to assure her that the royal permission to dedicate meant exactly what it said, but also to make some suggestions of his own about a suitable subject for her next book. Would she delineate, in some future work, the habits of Life and Character and Enthusiasm of a clergyman, who should pass his time between the metropolis and the country? It almost sounded as if he would be prepared to write it for her! It is easy to imagine the reaction of Jane and Henry to this missive.

When Jane eventually replied to Mr Clarke, she explained – doubtless with her tongue in her cheek – that she was honoured by the suggestion, but did not feel capable of taking it up. She wrote:

A classical education, or at any rate a very extensive acquaintance with English literature, ancient and modern, appears to me quite indispensable for the person who would do any justice to your clergyman; I think I may boast myself to be, with all possible vanity, the most unlearned and uninformed female who ever dared to be an authoress.

She was, of course, nothing of the kind, but much may be forgiven her in her attempts to put off the egregious Mr Clarke. He refused to be put off. He returned with another request for "an English clergyman after *your* fancy", – which fancy he obviously hoped would resemble himself as much as possible. He later took the opportunity, when conveying the Prince Regent's thanks for his presentation volumes, to inform her of his appointment as chaplain and private English secretary to the Prince of Coburg, future husband of Princess Charlotte, and to suggest "a historical romance illustrative of the history of the august House of Coburg". Jane Austen replied, congratulating him on his appointment and sending her sincere good wishes; her concluding paragraph was calculated to put an end, once and for all, to his solicitations.

I could no more write a romance than an epic poem. I could not sit seriously down to write a serious romance under any other motive than to save my life; and if it were indispensable for me to keep it up and never relax to laughing at myself or other people, I am sure I should be hung before I had finished the first chapter. No, I must keep to my own style and go on in my own way; and though I may never succeed again in that, I am convinced that I shall totally fail in any other.

This would indeed have been the end of the matter, and of the importunate Mr Clarke, had he not placed posterity for ever in his debt by inspiring Jane's *Plan of a Novel*. She derived so much amusement from his well-meant suggestions that she carried them out in a mock synopsis which is as funny as anything in the *Juvenilia*.

There can be little doubt that Jane was thankful to get back to Chawton. The strain of nursing her brother through his dangerous illness had told on her own health. She was tired and vaguely uneasy, but she was already living in the world of *Persuasion*, which she had begun during the previous summer. The year 1816 was a difficult one for her and for the rest of her family, but there is no hint of this in the autumnal beauty of *Persuasion*. It would never have its final revision. There are passages which break upon the atmosphere of the book with a jarring note, reminding one of those passages in Jane's letters which upset the critics of today.

Doubtless she would have removed them, given time, but time was running out. They only leave the novel a fraction short of perfection, and how minute that fraction is, compared with the living, breathing movement of the book. The illusion is complete. "Don't talk to me of the Duke of Monmouth," exclaimed Tennyson, when he visited Lyme Regis. "Show me the spot where Louisa Musgrove fell!"

It is popular to regard *Persuasion* as autobiographical, but Anne Elliot is not Jane Austen, any more than those admirable naval officers are her sailor brothers, or those pretty girls her nieces. Only at one point she speaks from an unmistakable depth of experience. After she had finished the book, she felt unsatisfied. Her nephew, James's son, Edward, said in his Memoir:

> . . . this weighed upon her mind, the more so probably on account of the weak state of her health, so that one night she retired to rest in very low spirits. But such depression was little in accordance with her nature and was soon shaken off. The next morning she awoke to more cheerful views and brighter inspiration; the sense of power revived, and imagination renewed its course. She cancelled the condemned chapter, and wrote two others, entirely different, instead.

It is to this "brighter inspiration" that we owe the conversation between Anne Elliot and Captain Harville which culminates in a passage which forever gives the lie to those who claim that Jane Austen never truly loved. "All the privilege I claim for my own sex (it is not a very enviable one, you need not covet it) is that of loving longest, when existence or when hope is gone."

12

"WE DO NOT grow older, of course," wrote Jane Austen, in a letter to her eleven-year-old niece, Caroline. Written in fun, this was true in a subtle way. Her letters were as delightful as ever, especially when addressed to the younger members of the family; she enjoyed her imaginary world and her career as an author; she entered into the concerns of the younger generation – Fanny's love affairs, Anna's pregnancies, Edward's ambitions, Caroline's stories, and little Cassy's problems. It is only as one reads between the lines that one notices a change. She misses Cassandra terribly now, when she is away from home; she enjoys the constant family invasions, but she worries about where to put them all and what to feed them on – "composition seems to me Impossible with a head full of Joints of Mutton and doses of rhubarb"; and just occasionally there is a reference to her health – "thank you, my Back has given me scarcely any pain for many days."

The difficulties of the post-war period must have had their repercussions on her health. The inevitable financial troubles following on the conclusion of a prolonged war had affected the business and banking world. Henry's serious illness in 1815 had been largely due to his business worries, and these had not been lessened by his absence from the bank. In March, 1816, the worst happened; the Alton bank failed and brought Austen, Maude and Tilson crashing down with it. The brilliant, lively, mercurial Henry was bankrupt. His brother Edward and his uncle James Leigh Perrot lost considerable sums of money; Madame Bigeon, the French house-keeper who had been in charge of his household since the early days of his marriage, lost all her savings; even Jane lost £13, which she could ill spare. It was over half her annual allowance of former days. The irrepressible Henry came up smiling, as he always did. He carried out his long-ago intention of taking Orders and by the end of the year was installed at Bentley, near Alton, where his sermons were much admired.

"Uncle Henry writes very superior sermons," wrote Jane to her nephew Edward at Steventon, who had recently embarked on a novel. "You and I must try to get hold of one or two, and put them into our Novels: – it would be a fine help to a volume; and we could make our Heroine read it aloud of a Sunday evening." Edward had lost two and a half chapters of his manuscript, and in condoling with him, his aunt gave an oft-quoted description of her own manner of work.

> It is well that I have not been at Steventon lately and therefore cannot be suspected of purloining them: two strong twigs and a half towards a Nest of my own, would have been something. – I do not think however that any theft of that sort would be really useful to me. What should I do with your strong, manly, spirited sketches, full of Variety and Glow? – How could I possibly join them on to the little bit (two inches wide) of ivory on which I work with so fine a Brush as produces little effect after much labour?

Before leaving London, Henry was able to carry out a cherished plan which was to give him and his sister Jane much pleasure. He went to the office of the dilatory publisher, Crosby, and asked for the manuscript of *Susan*. Not unless he repaid the original ten pounds they said firmly. Henry produced the required sum, and the manuscript was duly found and returned to him. Then, and not until then, Henry informed the publisher that the manuscript which had been neglected for so long was by the author of *Pride and Prejudice*.

Jane changed the heroine's name to Catherine and carried out a little revision, but somehow the work flagged. She was working on *Persuasion*, and in the back of her mind another story was stirring. For the time being she put aside the book which was later to be known as *Northanger Abbey*: "Miss Catherine is put upon the shelve for the present," she wrote to Fanny in March 1817, "and I do not know that she will ever come out."

Persuasion was finished in July, 1816, and ready to be worked over and revised. Writing to Fanny in the following March, Jane reckoned it should be ready for publication in "about a twelve-month". In her next letter, replying to some comment of Fanny's, she wrote: "You will not like it, so you need not be impatient. You may *perhaps* like the Heroine, as she is almost too good for me."

It has been popular for some people to see in *Persuasion* the swan song of Jane Austen. For them, her last published work seems to have a "dying fall", curving exquisitely downwards like a rainbow. One might believe this, were it not for *Sanditon*. The story that was already stirring in her mind, when she was working on *Persuasion*, came for a little while hilariously to life, and there was nothing of a swan song about it. It was robust and witty, with such a breath of sea air about it that you can almost taste the salt on your lips. Mr Parker is the grand-daddy of every modern developer who ever with the best of intentions ruined a quiet beauty spot; his hypochondriacal brother and sisters could be met with today at any fashionable health resort where so-called invalids discuss their imaginary ailments and criticize the National Health Service.

Charlotte Haywood, one of the two heroines (the other is the lovely, impecunious Clara Brereton), watches Arthur surreptitiously spreading extra butter on his warm toast and suspects that he is "determined on having no Disorders but such as called for warm rooms and good nourishment". Lady Denham, "born to wealth but not to education", can keep all her relations at her beck and call, for she has "many thousands a year to bequeath and three distinct sets of people to be courted by". When Jane had discussed the title of the book with Cassandra, she was considering *The Brothers*, but when the unfinished work was published, the family called it *Sanditon*.

Jane's sense of place was vivid: we can walk through the grounds of Pemberley and fish in Mr Darcy's trout stream; we can open a door on the main street of Highbury and see it through Emma's eyes.

> Emma went to the door for amusement. Much could not be hoped from the traffic of even the busiest part of Highbury; – Mr. Perry walking hastily by; Mr. William Cox letting himself in at the office door; Mr. Cole's carriage-horses returning from exercise; or a stray letter-boy on an obstinate mule, were the liveliest objects she could presume to expect; and when her eyes fell only on the butcher with his tray, a tidy old woman travelling homewards from shop with her full basket, two curs quarrelling over a dirty bone, and a string of dawdling children round the baker's little bow-window eyeing the gingerbread, she knew she had no reason to complain, and was amused enough: quite enough still to stand at the door.

We can recapture the atmosphere of Lyme Regis and Bath as Jane Austen knew them, and overhear Admiral Croft's observations on the passers-by, as he turns away from that print-shop window, where he has been criticizing some uninspired artist's idea of a boat: "There comes old Sir Archibald Drew and his grandson. Look, he sees us; he kisses his hand to you; he takes you for my wife. Ah! the peace has come too soon for that younker." All these we can see as the stories unfold, but as for *Sanditon*, we can hardly read a word without being conscious of the sea.

During these months of insidious ill-health, Jane Austen never failed to keep up her correspondence with her nephews and nieces. She wrote a letter to Charles's little Cassy with all the words spelt backwards, a task which must have taken up time she could ill spare, but one can imagine the delight of the child on receiving it. She would write to Caroline about her stories, often adding little messages purporting to come from the piano: "The piano Forté often talks of you; in various keys, tunes and expressions I allow — but be it Lesson, or Country Dance, Sonata or Waltz, *you* are really its constant Theme. I wish you could come and see us, as easily as Edward can." Caroline was musical as well as imaginative, and she enjoyed playing the piano when she visited her grandmother and her aunts. Increasingly Jane wrote to Edward, Caroline's brother, who was becoming a favourite nephew, and she still carried on a lively correspondence with Fanny about her love affairs. "You are inimitable, irresistible," wrote Jane, in the February of 1817:

> You are the delight of my Life. Such Letters, such entertaining Letters as you have lately sent! . . . You can hardly think what a pleasure it is to me, to have such thorough pictures of your Heart. — Oh! what a loss it will be when you are married. You are too agreeable in your single state, too agreeable as a Neice. . . . Single Women have a dreadful propensity for being poor — which is one very strong argument in favour of Matrimony, but I need not dwell on such arguments with *you*, pretty Dear, you do not want inclination. — Well, I shall say, as I have often

said before, Do not be in a hurry; depend upon it, the right Man will come at last.

Fanny, with a more sensitive understanding of her aunt than might have been expected of a young girl, went on writing those entertaining letters even when she was desperately anxious about Jane's increasing illness. It was the one remaining thing she could do for her, and she went on doing it to the end.

Jane Austen's illness seemed to fluctuate, and nobody could tell what was causing it. Sometimes she would be bilious and feverish; sometimes her back would ache and she would be unable to walk; sometimes her pretty complexion would be blotched with dark patches. At other times she seemed suddenly to recover. In a letter to Charles she wrote:

> I was so ill on Friday and thought myself so likely to be worse that I could not but press for Cassandra's return with Frank after the Funeral last night, which she of course did, and either her return, or my having seen Mr. Curtis, or my Disorder's chusing to go away, have made me better this morning.

The funeral mentioned in this letter was that of Uncle James Leigh Perrot; his will brought disappointment to Mrs Austen, for she was not mentioned in it. Thinking he would surely outlive his sister, who was so often ailing, he settled his entire fortune on his wife for her lifetime; on her death, James would inherit everything, with the exception of one thousand pounds apiece for those of his nephews and nieces who survived their aunt. Jane felt the disappointment keenly and was ashamed of herself for doing so. It brought on a relapse, and she confessed as much to Charles. "I am the only one of the legatees who has been so silly, but a weak Body must excuse weak Nerves." It was typical of her that she added a postscript for the children, with a special message for a delicate child. "Tell dear Harriet that if she wants me in her service again, she must send a Hackney Chariot all the way for me, for I am not strong enough to travel any other way, and I hope Cassy will take care that it is a green one."

There were no more walks to Alton and back, though sometimes on her better days she would ride out on one of the donkeys, with Cassandra and young Edward walking by her side. Soon even this was too much for her, and she would spend the day on a makeshift sofa, contrived from three chairs placed together. She would not lie on the only sofa in the house because her mother always used it, and she thought her need was the greater.

One day in April, 1817, when twelve-year-old Caroline was staying with Anna and Ben at Wyards, the two sisters walked over to Chawton to ask after their Aunt Jane. She was unable to leave her room, but she was eager to see them, so Anna and Caroline went upstairs and found her sitting in an armchair, wearing her dressing gown. "She got up and kindly greeted us – and then pointing to the seats which had been arranged for us by the fire, she said, 'This is a chair for the married lady and a little stool for you, Caroline.' It is strange, but those trifling words are the last of hers that I can remember." They did not stay long; Aunt Cassandra beckoned them away. "I do not suppose we stayed a quarter of an hour," wrote Caroline, "and I never saw Aunt Jane again."

Not many people saw Aunt Jane again. The members of her family were becoming increasingly anxious and alarmed. Cassandra and Martha nursed her devotedly; her mother was worried and distressed; anxious enquiries poured in from her brothers – "Every dear brother so devoted and so anxious!" she wrote in one of her last letters. She was upheld in the love of the whole family. "In short, if I live to be an old Woman, I must expect to wish I had died now, blessed in the tenderness of such a Family and before I had survived either them or their affection."

Mr. Curtis was at a loss to explain the cause of her illness or to effect a cure. In the end Mr Lyford of Winchester Hospital was called in, and it was decided to move her to lodgings at Winchester, where she might be under his care. Cassandra would go with her, of course. Their old friends, Alethea Bigg and her widowed sister, Mrs Heathcote, were now living in Winchester, so they would have friends close at hand, though Alethea was away in Switzerland when they arrived.

They set off for Winchester on a wild, wet day in May. James and Mary lent their carriage for the journey, and Henry and her nephew William (one of Edward's sons) rode one at each side of the carriage. It distressed her to think of them riding stoically in the rain. Possibly Mrs Austen and Martha Lloyd stood at the door, watching them go. The sound of the horses' hoofs receded and all was quiet. The house itself was quiet. Something of its life was gone, never to return. The child Caroline's words would echo eternally through those quiet rooms – the writing desk forever closed, the piano silent, the "light that never was on sea or land" faded, the laughter stilled – "I never saw Aunt Jane again."

Epilogue

I SOMETIMES WONDER if my great-great-grandfather, William Curtis, saw that carriage being driven away towards Winchester through the pouring rain. On the whole, I doubt it. But I am very sure that he knew what the end of the journey would be, and that his patient was being carried swiftly towards that "undiscovered country from whose bourne No traveller returns".

I remember my indignation, many years ago, when I read in some article on Jane Austen that her illness was beyond the simple skill of the apothecary in Alton, who could not even discover what it was. Nor could anybody else, as recent research has proved. In the *British Medical Journal* for 18 July 1964, Dr (later Sir) Zachary Cope, after a careful study of the symptoms as described in her letters, diagnozed it as Addison's Disease, a disease of the adrenal glands which was not identified until long after her death. In her day, it was incurable; today it can be treated by injection.

There is a tradition in the Curtis family that Jane Austen had William Curtis in mind when she created Mr Perry in *Emma* – Mr Perry on whose judgement Mr Woodhouse relied so implicitly. I like to think it may have been so, for then my great-grandmother must have been one of the little Perrys, who were seen in the High Street eating slices of Mrs Weston's wedding cake. I always imagine them outside the old Curtis house in Alton, though Highbury is supposed to have been Leatherhead. Jane must often have seen them as she walked into Alton from Chawton, or came rattling up the steep street in the donkey cart. I sometimes look up at my great-grandmother's serene face in her portrait, and ask: "Did you really see Jane Austen? Didn't you know who she was? Surely you must have known all about her by the time you married my great-grandfather Crowley and moved across the road to Normandy House, where your children were born. Why didn't you tell them about her? Why? – Why? – Why?"

Perhaps it is as well there is no answer. Perhaps the little Curtises thought she was rather a funny lady, with a troublesome old mother who was always sending for their father urgently at all sorts of odd hours. When he had galloped out to Chawton in haste, he would find nothing much wrong with her – she might even be digging potatoes in the garden. After all, what did Mrs Perry and the little Perrys think of dear Mr Woodhouse?

My great-great-grandfather must have continued to visit the house in Chawton, to attend on Mrs Austen, and Cassandra, and Martha Lloyd. Mrs Austen lived to a great age. "I sometimes think that God Almighty must have forgotten me," she would say. "But I dare say he will come for me in His own good time." She died in 1827, at the age of eighty-eight. A year later, Martha left Chawton to be married to Frank, now a widower, and to be a mother to his family. Cassandra never married; during her later years she spent much time with Frank, now an admiral – both the sailor brothers became admirals.

When Cassandra died, in 1845, she was brought to lie beside her mother in the churchyard at Chawton. As I stood there recently, looking at the two simple headstones, I found myself wishing that there could have been a third, and that Jane might have been laid beside them. All that rich life of hers belongs to Chawton rather than to Winchester, where she longed for "nothing but death". Only, of course, for such as Jane Austen, death can have no dominion. She is part of the living heritage of England.

Chapman, R. W. (editor) *Jane Austen's Letters* 2nd edition, reprinted with corrections, Oxford University Press, 1969

Chapman, R. W. (editor) *Jane Austen; Facts and Problems* Oxford University Press, 1948

Halpern, John (editor) *Jane Austen Bicentenary Essays* Cambridge University Press, 1975

Hodge, Jane Aiken *The Double Life of Jane Austen* Hodder & Stoughton, 1972

Jenkins, Elizabeth *Jane Austen: A Biography* Gollancz, 1938 (hardback); Cardinal, 1973 (paperback)

Kennedy, Margaret *Jane Austen* Barker, 1950 (out-of-print, but available in libraries)

Lascelles, Mary *Jane Austen and Her Art* Oxford University Press, 1939; Oxford paperback, 1963

Laski, Marghanita *Jane Austen and Her World* Thames & Hudson, 1969

Pinion, F. B. *A Jane Austen Companion* Macmillan, 1973

Wright, Andrew *Jane Austen's Novels* Chatto & Windus, 1953 (hardback); Penguin, 1962 (paperback)